Educational Systems
in the United States

THE LIBRARY OF EDUCATION

A Project of The Center for Applied Research in Education, Inc.

G. R. Gottschalk, Director

Categories of Coverage

I	II	III
Curriculum and Teaching	Administration, Organization, and Finance	Psychology for Educators

IV	V	VI
History, Philosophy, and Social Foundations	Professional Skills	Educational Institutions

Educational Systems in the United States

WILLIAM W. BRICKMAN

*Professor of Educational History and
Comparative Education
Graduate School of Education
University of Pennsylvania*

The Center for Applied Research in Education, Inc.
New York

Foreword

Unique among the nations of the world, the United States has no national program of education. Nowhere in the federal Constitution is the term *education* to be found. Since its inception, however, no nation has been as committed to education as our republic.

The foundation for this commitment to education, which is local and state centered, is reflected in the country's elementary and secondary schools, public and private, which enroll upwards of 90 per cent of the youth of school age, an accomplishment no other nation can claim. Here in *Educational Systems in the United States,* another distinguished contribution in the Library of Education series, Dr. William W. Brickman, an able, brilliant, and authoritative educational writer, discusses their origin, purpose, growth, and development.

Admitting that the independent, church-related, parochial, and public school complex makes for a dualism in the educational enterprise, the author argues that strength rather than weakness results. The pattern is indigenous to the pluralism which is characteristic of our national scheme of things. It has contributed to our national purpose and greatness. In it unity through diversity is expressed.

Schools other than those which are tax supported should, in the opinion of Dr. Brickman, be regarded as "quasi-public or semi-public." Like the public schools these institutions "perform a public service by educating young Americans for a useful life in their communities and in the nation at large, and because they are controlled, even if not supported, by the public educational authorities."

There is, of course, obvious validity in the assertion that "the history of education in the United States is the history of public *and* independent education" and that "both elements in the dual system of education in America have demonstrated their ability to contribute to the national welfare." At a time when national policy regarding all education is in the making, the author's assertion that "both need strengthening but not at the expense of each other" will continue to be argued and debated.

To that argument and debate this volume is certain to contribute basic and authoritative background information, and, in presenting the dualism of American elementary and secondary education in historical, social, political, and economic perspective, will be helpful in clarifying issues and in determining judgments. It is opportune and timely.

HEROLD C. HUNT
Charles William Eliot
Professor of Education
Harvard University

Educational Systems
in the United States

William W. Brickman

Whenever anyone thinks of American education he seems, inevitably, to think only of the public schools. From the Colonial period on, however, there have been elementary and secondary schools supported by private funds. These include the independent, church-related, and parochial schools. Professor Brickman conceptualizes all of the American lower schools as the "dual system of education." This volume presents the origin, development, and organization of the dual system. The conflicts between the public and private elements concerning federal aid, church-state relations, the existence of private schools, and racial segregation are presented in succinct form.

This book forms a trilogy with *Organization of Public Schools* by Wynn and *Federal, State, and Local Government in Education* by Pierce. Together these three Library of Education volumes give a complete picture of the organization of public education in the United States.

Dr. William Brickman is Professor of Educational History and Comparative Education in the Graduate School of Education at the University of Pennsylvania. He is a prolific writer, a world traveler, and a thoroughly competent scholar.

DANIEL E. GRIFFITHS
Content Editor

Contents

CHAPTER I

Historical Background of
Public and Private Education

Education in America aims to bring about the fullest possible development of each individual in accordance with his abilities, interests, and needs, as well as to make him a well-informed member of his community and nation. To understand fully the nature, functions, and role of the elementary and secondary school system in the United States, it is first necessary to know how it came about. Many of the current educational problems are deeply rooted in the events of the past, and historical analysis is very helpful in comprehending current issues.

European Traditions

It is possible to trace American ideas and practices in education to the very sources of European civilization—ancient Palestine, the Greco-Roman world, and early Christianity. There is a direct link between the religious content in American schools and the thoughts expressed in the Old and New Testament. *The New England Primer,* the textbook which was widely used during the eighteenth century and part of the nineteenth, began with a quotation from the Book of Proverbs: "Train up a child in the way he should go and when he is old he will not depart from it." A prominent place was reserved in this popular book for the Lord's Prayer and for the Westminster Catechism, essential elements in the education of young Protestants. From ancient Greece and Rome were derived the classical languages and literatures which occupied an important place in the curriculum of the secondary school and college for a long period in American history.

The more direct origins of American education can be found in the period of the Protestant Reformations and the Catholic Counter-Reformation during the sixteenth and early seventeenth centuries.

1

According to Martin Luther, the governmental authority in Germany furthered the cause of religion in education by passing legislation for compulsory school attendance. Similarly, John Calvin of Geneva inaugurated a religious reform movement which emphasized universal knowledge of Scripture, but which separated the state and the church. Both reforms had an impact in colonial America: Lutheranism chiefly in Pennsylvania, and Calvinism in New England (Congregationalism), New Netherlands (Dutch Reformed Church), and other areas (Presbyterianism). In each instance, the European religious groups put their educational ideas into practice in the New World. The Anglican Reformation, the source of educational ideas and practice in such colonies as New York, provided the impetus for the second American institution of higher learning, the College of William and Mary (1693).

The educational activities in North America outside the English colonies were under the auspices of the Catholic Church, which aimed to regain religious supremacy over the Protestants. Eventually, the Catholics opened schools in the Protestant areas, and these schools were conducted by members of religious orders—Jesuits, Christian Brothers, and Ursuline Sisters—founded during the Catholic Counter-Reformation.

The educational features of the countries from which the colonists came have been the models for the early American schools. Although England did not, in the seventeenth century, provide a formal education for the common people, it had already taken some steps for the promotion of apprenticeship schooling. In general, England had an outline of a formal school system: elementary and writing schools, Latin grammar schools, and the Universities of Oxford and Cambridge. The universities were not so much centers of advanced intellectual labor as training schools for future clergymen of the Church of England.

Early American education also derived directly from the Scottish and Dutch school systems. The Scottish system stressed universal education, local school administration, and the certification and supervision of teachers by the church authorities; the latter Dutch system had primary schools under the joint control of the church and the municipal authorities, Latin Grammar Schools supported and supervised by the towns, and three universities. The order by the Synod of Dort (1619) for the establishment of schools with religious instruction in all Dutch villages—with local support, control by church authorities, and free teaching of poor children—seemed to foreshadow colonial American practice, even if a direct influence cannot be easily demonstrated.

The Colonial Period

The first educational work in the colonies was conducted in the home. As life and society became more complex, education was increasingly carried on by other agencies. Early records are rather scarce, but there was concern for education in line with the demands of religious ideology. The Virginia charter of 1606, which preceded by one year the founding of Jamestown, mentioned the need of the "propagating of Christian religion" to the natives, and it seems probable that there was a similar provision at least for the education of the settlers' own children. But actual schools seemed to have been planned at first for the Indians only, with some specific action being taken toward the establishment of a "University and College" at Henrico, Virginia, in 1618. Shortly afterward, an effort was made to open the East India School so that the children of the settlers would not have to be sent to England for a systematic education. Even the Indian revolt of March, 1622, could not put an end to these experiments, but rather seemed to spur the colonists on.

Apprenticeship training was common in all the colonies. In 1642 Virginia and Massachusetts passed important legislation along these lines, with the latter ordering the town authorities to make certain that children were trained "to read and understand the principles of religion and the capitall lawes of this country." Earlier, a Virginia law of 1631 required ministers to teach children, youth, and "ignorant persons" to read the Ten Commandments and the Catechism; but it was the Old Deluder Satan Act of 1647, passed by the General Court of Massachusetts, which seemed to set the tone for American education. This act ordered townships with fifty families each to appoint a teacher of reading and writing who would be paid from public funds. It also ordered townships of one hundred families each to open a grammar school which would prepare youth for higher education. An interesting aspect of both Massachusetts laws was the principle of a monetary fine for noncompliance. The aim of the 1647 act was frankly religious: to defeat the designs of the devil who kept men from the study of the Scriptures. This law also included three basic principles of the present American system of public education: local finance, local administration, and the line of demarcation between elementary school and secondary school.

The Old Deluder Satan Act was re-echoed in the legislative halls of all the New England colonies with the exception of Rhode Island, where the principle of private education prevailed. All through the colonial period, private and public schools existed side by side. When the famous Boston Latin School, which was supported by public funds, was founded in 1635, it was already preceded by private schools established not long after the settlement of the town.

A common form of private education was the dame school, generally taught by a woman of meager knowledge and ability. Yet, boys and girls did learn the elements of reading (by means of the hornbook) and, in some cases, rudimentary arithmetic and writing. The apprenticeship system provided private instruction in trades and even in the reading of Scripture and in writing. On a higher level, there were private grammar schools in several colonies. In 1638 was founded the Collegiate School of New York City, the oldest existing private secondary school in the country.[1] Roxbury Latin School, West Roxbury, Massachusetts, has been in operation since 1645; Hopkins Grammar School, New Haven, Connecticut, since 1660; and the William Penn Charter School, Philadelphia, Pennsylvania, since 1689.

Helpful as the private schools were in the establishment of educational facilities, they could not accomplish what the town schools were able to do. In these publicly supported and publicly controlled schools, the teachers were paid through tax levies and were supervised by the town government or by the education committee, the precursor of the school board. During much of the colonial period the governmental and the religious authorities cooperated in the supervision of the schools.

With the growth of the population in New England, new types of schools began to appear. In the eighteenth century there arose the "moving school," actually the designation for a teacher who taught for several months in the villages near the town. This school

---

[1] Ernest B. Chamberlain, *Our Independent Schools: The Private School in Education* (New York: American Book Company, 1944), p. 44.

was the ancestor of the district school in the rural areas of New England and elsewhere in the country. Even if the district school was not regarded as offering a good education, it did perform a useful service by providing the educational foundations of many children.

Perhaps the most popular medium of elementary instruction in the colonies was the *New England Primer,* apparently first published in Boston in 1690. The reputation of this textbook, which was of English origin, was that "it taught millions to read and not one to sin." The three million copies in slightly different versions taught the alphabet, spelling, reading, and catechism. The method of teaching the alphabet was particularly interesting, as it was done by means of rhymes. For example:

In Adam's Fall	The idle Fool
We sinned all	Is whipt at School

The *New England Primer,* with its simple woodcuts, could be found in American schools until about the mid-nineteenth century, when its leading place was taken by Noah Webster's blue-backed *American Spelling Book,* issued in its original form in 1783.

The opening of the Boston Latin School in 1635 marked the start of public secondary education in New England. This and other grammar schools stressed instruction in Latin and Greek language and literature by able scholars, such as Ezekiel Cheever, who taught for some seventy years in various towns. Under such masters, selected boys were able to qualify for higher study at Harvard College.

The rapid changes in society, ideas, industry, and commerce in the middle of the eighteenth century gave birth to a new school, the academy, which was favored by such men as Benjamin Franklin. The academy laid stress on modern and practical subjects and therefore enjoyed a popular appeal. Essentially a privately financed school, the academy reflected the changing era and contributed in many ways to the welfare of the new nation. For one thing, it pointed the way to the system of public schools in the nineteenth century, in particular to the necessity for trained teachers. Moreover, the academy movement resulted in the establishment of such influential private schools as Governor Dummer Academy (1761), Phillips Andover (1778) and Phillips Exeter (1783) Academies, and Deerfield Academy (1797).

The lag between the traditional offerings of the Latin grammar schools and the desires of many people for a modernized curriculum led to the founding of private schools in Boston and in other large cities during the eighteenth century. Thus, Owen Harris' school in Boston taught geometry, astronomy, surveying, and navigation, while Isaac Greenwood's school offered geography, algebra, and conic sections in 1727, and history in 1734. There were even opportunities in the evening for those occupied by day.

Early in the eighteenth century, the public authorities of Boston passed laws requiring that the private schoolmasters had to be approved by town and church authorities. Under such circumstances, the quality of instruction in the private schools was supposed to be the same as that in the publicly financed schools.

The earliest Catholic school was founded in Maryland in 1640, and the first Jewish day school was opened in 1731 in New York City for instruction in sacred and secular subjects. Other private religious schools with secular courses were founded during the colonial period by the Quakers, Lutherans, and Episcopalians.

Since society in the Middle Colonies was characterized by religious pluralism, there were different school programs. In New Netherlands, the Dutch burghers organized public schools in which the three R's and religion were taught. The English period, beginning in 1664, saw the opening of schools for the poor by the Society for the Propagation of the Gospel in Foreign Parts, an Anglican organization founded in 1701 in England. In addition to grammar schools preparing boys for King's College (Columbia), New York City had private day and evening schools. John Walton's evening school in New York City offered in 1723 a typical private-school curriculum: the three R's, Latin, Greek, Hebrew, navigation, surveying, rhetoric, metaphysics, and other subjects.

One of the significant achievements of the private religious schools in the Middle Colonies was the publication in 1770 of the first book on education in the colonies—Christopher Dock's *Schul-Ordnung* (School Management). Another significant contribution was the opening in 1689 of the Friends' Public School (actually private) of Philadelphia, the original name of the William Penn Charter School. The Academy of Philadelphia, described in 1743 by Benjamin Franklin and opened in 1751, was divided into three departments: Latin, English, and Mathematics. The Latin Department developed into the University of Pennsylvania. In addition to instruction in modern languages, sciences, geography, and history, Franklin's Academy also made provision "that a number of the poorer Sort will be hereby qualified to act as schoolmasters in the Country."

The colonial school policy in the South was laissez-faire in contrast to the compulsory school maintenance of New England and the parochial school organization of the Middle Colonies. Because of their peculiar geographical, social, and economic situation, the Southern colonies set up a system of laws for the apprentice training of the orphaned and of the children of the poor, as well as charity schools, tutoring and private schools for the rich, and Old Field Schools on abandoned land in rural districts. Wills and bequests often yielded an endowment for a school. The Syms-Eaton School in Virginia, for example, was started with the will of Benjamin Syms in 1634 and was expanded by the will of Thomas Eaton in 1659. Negro children were given some education whenever plantation owners were concerned with the inculcation of Christianity.

In secondary education the South could boast of some schools. The best known was King William's School, opened in 1696 at Annapolis, Maryland, by the General Assembly as a free public school. About a century later, this institution became known as St. John's College. Among the academies in the South, Zion Parnassus Academy, Salisbury, North Carolina, established by the Rev. Samuel Eusebius McCorkle in 1785, was noted for its pioneering experiment with teacher training.

The American Revolution (1776–81) temporarily interrupted educational activity in various parts of North America. The new idea of universal education was expressed in plans for the expansion of educational opportunity. In 1779, Thomas Jefferson introduced into the Virginia legislature his Bill for the More General Diffusion of Knowledge, providing for a three-level public school system. According to Jefferson, this bill would bring to all the children of the state a minimum program of the three R's, while the superior pupils would have opportunities for secondary and higher education. This revolutionary reform, however, was not approved by the legislature. In 1786, Dr. Benjamin Rush proposed to the Pennsylvania legislature one system of education which would be free and publicly supported. These men and others were conscious of the relations between public education and citizenship, freedom, and democracy.

By 1789, the new state constitutions of Pennsylvania, North Carolina, Georgia, Vermont, Massachusetts, and New Hampshire had made provisions for public schools. On the national level, Congress passed the Land Ordinance of 1785, reserving a parcel of territory, Section Sixteen, in each township in the Western lands for the maintenance of public schools. The Northwest Ordinance of July 13, 1787, stated: ". . . religion, morality, and knowledge, being necessary to good government and the happiness of mankind, schools and the means of education shall forever be encouraged."

As the new nation was being born, public schools could be said to have been in existence in the New England states only. School standards were generally low, except in Massachusetts and Connecticut. Apprentice training declined as a result of the new political, economic, and social forces. Religious groups maintained charity schools for the poor. The time seemed ripe for a more definite and comprehensive plan of public education. In fact, New York State organized a public school system in 1784 and reorganized it three years later. Known as the University of the State of New York, it comprised all kinds of schools in accordance with the French precedent of centralized administration.

The New Republic, 1789–1837

The Constitution of the United States of America was silent on the subject of education. On the basis of the Tenth Amendment, education became a function of the several states. Nevertheless, the federal government, because of the "general welfare" clause in the Constitution and the doctrine of implied governmental powers, has given billions of dollars for all kinds of educational projects, such as the Office of Education, the Library of Congress, and agricultural and vocational education.

The lack of a national educational system did not deter thoughtful Americans from forging plans for a unified system. In 1795, the American Philosophical Society organized an essay contest to obtain the best blueprint for a uniquely American system of public education. Among those who submitted plans were Benjamin Rush, Robert Coram, Du Pont de Nemours (an expatriate Frenchman),

Samuel H. Smith, and Samuel Knox. The writers agreed that a national culture requires a nationwide school system, and most favored universal, free education for both boys and girls.

After 1800, public-minded citizens took note of the defects which were prevalent in the charity or pauper schools in the Middle and the Southern states: inadequate facilities, small attendance, no supervision or control, and inconsistency with the ideals of a developing democratic society. An improvement was evident to some extent with the organization in 1805 of the Free School Society of New York. The charity schools (opened by the funds collected under the auspices of this group, which changed its name to Public School Society in 1826) made possible educational opportunities to the underprivileged. When the Society was merged with the New York City Board of Education in 1852, it could look back with satisfaction upon almost a half century of fruitful educational activity: the education of more than 600,000 children by 1200 teachers in 115 schools.

The work of the voluntary organizations was made possible largely through the medium of the monitorial method of instruction, which was developed independently by two Englishmen, the Rev. Andrew Bell and Joseph Lancaster. Monitorial instruction involved one teacher who prepared young pupil teachers who, in turn, taught the same lesson to hundreds of children. This system was first introduced into America in 1806 in New York, and then into other cities. For at least four to five decades, this procedure for the education of many children at a trifling cost constituted a step toward universal education. As a private, experimental venture, it showed, by contrast, that better forms of education under public control were possible. As in other instances in the history of American education, private effort showed the way to the public schools.

President George Washington's Farewell Address in 1796 emphasized the significance of education in a democracy: "Promote, then, as an object of primary importance, institutions for the general diffusion of knowledge. In proportion as the structure of a government gives force to public opinion, it is essential that public opinion should be enlightened." [2] According to Governor De Witt Clinton of New York State, the encouragement of education was the first

---

[2] James D. Richardson, ed., *Messages and Papers of the Presidents, 1789–1897, Vol. I* (Washington, D.C.: Government Printing Office, 1896), pp. 213–23.

duty and the best evidence of good government. Some said, "Open a school and close a jail." Others connected a proper education with teaching ability, often citing the slogan, "As is the teacher, so is the school."

Labor groups in particular exerted political pressure for schools in line with their conviction that a strong public educational system would aid economic and social growth in a democratic society. Other proponents of public schools included educators: James Gordon Carter and Horace Mann of Massachusetts, Henry Barnard of Connecticut, and Archibald D. Murphey of North Carolina. These men edited periodicals, made speeches, visited European schools to obtain new ideas and inspiration, and otherwise carried on intensive propaganda for a public school system. All these efforts and the growing movement for democracy in the Jacksonian spirit yielded positive results.

The drive for state systems of public education was closely related to the campaigns for the raising of funds for schools. At first, lotteries were authorized in most of the states and in the District of Columbia, but, as public morality grew more sensitive, this method of financing tended to disappear. Instead, new procedures were adopted: rate bills, or tuition charges based on the number of children of the family in school; and local taxes, as required by the Massachusetts Law of 1827. The more progressive states established permanent school funds through the sale of public lands (Connecticut in 1795), marriage and tavern license fees (Delaware), the sale of slaves (Florida), fines and confiscations (Connecticut), state bank profits (Kentucky), state lotteries (New York, Rhode Island, Georgia, and North Carolina), and direct appropriations. During the battle for free state schools, Massachusetts abolished the rate bills in 1827, and Delaware did the same two years later. Other states, however, managed to hold on to this practice for decades.

New York State reorganized its school administration in 1787 to include secondary schools. All schools in New York State came under the supervision of the governmental authority, according to a law of 1812 which created the first state superintendency of common schools. The superintendent was "to digest and prepare plans for the improvement and management of the common school fund, and for the better organization of common schools." He was also "generally to perform all such services relative to the welfare of the schools, as he shall be directed to perform. . . ." [3] Although the first superintendent, Gideon Hawley, a capable and successful administrator, was discharged on political grounds in 1821, the duties of the office were carried out by the Secretary of State until the re-establishment of the state superintendency in 1854. The first permanent organization for the state control of education took place in 1837, when Horace Mann was chosen secretary of the State Board of Education of Massachusetts.

The methods of teaching in the elementary schools of the early nineteenth century were mainly those of recitation by individual pupils, repetitions, and memorization. The textbook was usually the sole source of knowledge. A widely used textbook in the spirit of the new republic was Noah Webster's *Grammatical Institutes of the English Language* (1783), which covered spelling, reading, and grammar. The first part of this work was called the *American Spelling Book,* but its popular designation was the "Old Blue Back." Its impact on national education may be judged, in part, from the sale of over 5,000,000 copies by 1818 and 24,000,000 by 1847. An advertisement in the edition of 1848 claimed a sale "throughout the United States and Canada, exceeding One Million Copies Annually." [4] In 1921, an historian testified, "Its total sales by this time probably exceed seventy-five million and it is still selling by the hundred thousand a year in spite of a thousand competitors which have sprung up since its publication." [5] Another significant contribution by Webster was his *Compendious Dictionary of the English Language,* which has been a source of linguistic knowledge from 1806 to the present.

Lindley Murray prepared more scholarly books for the teaching of grammar, reading, and spelling. Jedediah Morse produced texts in geography; Peter Parley (Samuel G. Goodrich), in geography

---

[3] Thomas E. Finegan, *Free Schools: A Documentary History of the Free School Movement in New York State* (Albany, N.Y.: University of the State of New York, 1921), pp. 43–44.

[4] Noah Webster, *The Elementary Spelling Book: Being an Improvement on the American Spelling Book* (New York: G. F. Cooledge and Brother, 1848). Inside the front cover the last five words are in bold type. Webster designed his book not merely as a tool for language learning, but also as a medium of "just ideas of religion, morals and domestic economy." See Noah Webster, *The American Spelling Book* (Albany, N.Y.: Websters and Skinners, 1817), p. vi.

[5] Edwin E. Slosson, *The American Spirit in Education: A Chronicle of Great Teachers* (New Haven, Conn.: Yale University Press, 1921), p. 119.

and history; Warren Colburn and Nicholas Pike, in arithmetic; and Lowell Mason, in music. The first of the influential series of readers by Professor William Holmes McGuffey appeared in 1836.

The elementary school taught several new subjects, such as grammar, geography, history, physiology, and drawing. Moral teachings were given in a religious spirit, and Catholic, Jewish, and some Protestant groups found it necessary to establish schools of their own in an attempt to avoid the sectarian teaching in the public schools. In general, the early elementary school allowed the child more freedom than he had ever had and limited or abolished corporal punishment.

The new spirit in education was especially evident in some private schools. The Round Hill School, founded in 1823 by two scholars, George Bancroft and Joseph G. Cogswell, in Northampton, Massachusetts, stressed the significance of gymnastics. A. Bronson Alcott, a proponent of Pestalozzian pedagogical principles, opened a school in Cheshire, Connecticut, in 1825 and, from 1834 to 1839, conducted the Temple School in Boston. The latter might indeed be regarded as a precursor of the Progressive school of the twentieth century.

The private school provided competition to the public school, but it was the latter which became, in due course, the means by which the vast majority of Americans were educated. The public school was set up, furthermore, despite opposition to school taxes by property owners, expressions of fear of the government's power, and indifference by key leaders in public life.

The movement for secondary education under public auspices began when the Boston School Committee opened the English Classical School (later English High School) in 1821. In 1827, a Massachusetts law required every town or district of 500 families to open a tax-supported high school for the teaching of American history, geometry, surveying, and other subjects. All cities or towns with 4000 inhabitants were required to add instruction in Latin, Greek, history, rhetoric, and logic.

There was private initiative in other forms and aspects of education. In 1823, the Rev. Samuel Read Hall opened the first American normal school in Concord and published in 1829 the first native American textbook on pedagogy, *Lectures on Schoolkeeping*. James Gordon Carter, the "father of the normal school," started a private normal school in 1827 at Lancaster, Massachusetts. Both institutions foreshadowed the first public normal schools of more than a decade later. To the credit of private education are also Emma Hart Willard's Troy Female Seminary (1821) with its program of classical studies and teacher training, and Mary Lyon's Mt. Holyoke Seminary (1837)—two pioneering educational institutions for girls; Prudence Crandall's short-lived experiment in biracial education at Canterbury, Connecticut, between 1833 and 1838; the first school for deaf mutes, founded in 1817 in Hartford, Connecticut; the first school for the blind inaugurated in 1832 in Boston by John Fisher; and the inauguration of adult education by Josiah Holbrook's lyceum in 1826.

Education Reform and Expansion, 1837–65

Rapid growth of population, geographical area, and industrial and commercial activity took place before the Civil War. Several forces combined to bring about progress in education: pressures by labor, cultural, political, and educational leaders; pedagogical propaganda, such as William Russell's *American Journal of Education* (1826–31) and other periodicals; and the wave of humanitarianism. But there were also some retarding influences. Horace Mann attributed educational inefficiency and low standards to the law of 1789 legalizing the district school system and to the law of 1827 making this system compulsory. Mann extended school facilities, introduced supervision and in-service training of teachers, and increased teachers' salaries. However, his *Seventh Annual Report* (1843), which praised the pedagogical practices of Europe, aroused the educators of Boston, and his opposition to sectarian religion in the public schools angered the ministers, although Mann advocated Bible reading without comment. In denying that the public schools were anti-Christian or un-Christian, Mann affirmed that the Massachusetts system "invokes a religious spirit, and can never be fitly administered without such a spirit." [6]

Mann has justly been recognized as the most influential educational leader in nineteenth-century America, because his pioneering

---

[6] Horace Mann, *Twelfth Annual Report of the Board of Education, Together with the Twelfth Annual Report of the Secretary of the Board* (New York: E. P. Dutton & Co., Inc., 1849), p. 139.

reforms made a permanent impact on public education. His periodical, the *Common School Journal* (1838–48), was the inspiration for many another venture in educational journalism. He was chiefly responsible for the first public normal schools in America: at Lexington (1839) and at Barre and Bridgewater (1840). The power of his ideas influenced the work of the outstanding educational reformers in South America—Domingo Faustino Sarmiento of Argentina and José Pedro Varela of Uruguay.

The age of educational reform could boast of other educators of great stature, possibly at least one in each state. Henry Barnard, the counterpart of Mann in Connecticut and Rhode Island, edited the encyclopedic *American Journal of Education* (1855–82) and was the first U.S. Commissioner of Education (1867–70). Other educational statesmen included Calvin H. Wiley of North Carolina, Caleb Mills of Indiana, Samuel Lewis and Samuel Galloway of Ohio, John D. Pierce and Isaac E. Crary of Michigan, and John Swett of California.

Professional administration was extended around 1840 to the schools in counties and towns. The county superintendent was responsible for the assessment of taxes, the distribution of school funds, and the supervision of the public schools. The first city superintendency on a professional basis was established in 1839 with the appointment of Nathan Bishop as supervisor of the schools of Providence, Rhode Island. Of signal importance for the administration of public education was Massachusetts' enactment in 1852 of the first law for compulsory school attendance.

Massachusetts was also a pioneer in passing a law in 1857 for the admission to public schools of children without regard to "race, creed, or previous condition of servitude." The education of Negroes, sporadic in the North, had been forbidden by law in most of the Southern states since Nat Turner's rebellion in 1831.

The expansion of the high school coincided with the growing sentiment that secondary schooling was part of the public's responsibility for education. Central High School of Philadelphia, founded in 1838, was open to all qualified boys regardless of social class. The early curriculum was quite advanced, including civil engineering, astronomy, and logic. Before the Civil War, legal acceptance of the public high school had begun with court decisions in Indiana, Iowa, and Illinois recognizing the high school as a common school which could be supported from public funds.

In 1856, Mrs. Carl Schurz carried the ideas of the German educator Friedrich Froebel to Watertown, Wisconsin, establishing there a German-speaking kindergarten. A similar kindergarten was founded in 1858 at Columbus, Ohio, by Caroline Frankenburg. An English-speaking kindergarten was first opened in 1860 in Boston by Elizabeth Palmer Peabody. More than a decade later came the first public-school kindergarten.

Denominational schools also developed during 1837–65. The Presbyterians operated 264 parochial schools between 1845 and 1869. In 1855, the Episcopalians inaugurated St. Paul's, the famous preparatory school at Concord, New Hampshire. A number of Jewish day schools were functioning during the 1850's in New York City. The greatest spurt in sectarian education, however, was that made by the Catholics. The anti-Catholic sentiment and the resulting religious tension before mid-century led to a movement for separate Catholic schools. This idea had been urged by the First Provincial Council of 1829. The awareness of the essentially Protestant nature of the public schools prompted the Fourth Provincial Council in Baltimore in 1840 to order parish priests to prevent Catholic pupils in public schools from reading the King James Bible or singing Protestant hymns. After vainly seeking state funds for Catholic schools on the ground that the schools of the Public School Society of New York City were teaching Protestantism, Bishop John Hughes set up an independent Catholic school system after 1842. His action must have been an example to the First Plenary Council meeting in 1852 in Baltimore, which called upon all bishops to open a school in each parish and to use parish funds for teachers' salaries.

Toward a Dual School System, 1865–1900

The education and social welfare of the Negro received aid when Congress established the Freedmen's Bureau in 1865. For five years, the Bureau carried on various social and educational activities to raise the level of the Negro. All through the century, increasing educational opportunities, under public and private auspices, were made available to Negroes, but in the South the pattern of segregated education developed. The Morrill Land Grant Act, passed by Congress in 1862, aided agricultural and engineering training in the state colleges, as well as vocational training in the secondary schools. All attempts, however, at obtaining a general federal law for aid to the lower schools came to naught. Of some significance was the organization by the government of a Department (now Office) of Education in 1867—with Henry Barnard as the first commissioner —for the purpose of collecting and publishing data about education all over the country.

The larger city school systems were directed by a superintendent who reported to the central school board. In addition, city, county, and state systems were consolidated and expanded during the closing decades of the century. Subjects were added to curriculums in elementary and high schools; compulsory school attendance laws were put on the books; and appropriations were made in larger amounts for school buildings and teaching materials in response to the requirements of a rapidly rising population. The kindergarten found its way into the public school system when William Torrey Harris, superintendent of schools in St. Louis, introduced it in 1873.

New approaches were tried in elementary education with the application of the doctrines of Johann Heinrich Pestalozzi, as reinterpreted after 1860 by the Oswego Movement initiated by Edward A. Sheldon, superintendent of schools in Oswego, New York. Later, the pedagogical ideas of the prominent German philosopher, Johann Friedrich Herbart, were applied to the teaching of the social studies.

Francis W. Parker, superintendent of schools in Quincy, Massachusetts, and later principal of the Cook County Normal School in Chicago, and John Dewey in his Laboratory School at the University of Chicago (1896–1903) substituted methods based on child interest and needs for those of strict discipline and mechanical learning. Dewey was especially regarded as the inspirer of the Progressive education movement in the twentieth century.

The development of the high school was particularly significant for American education. The Kalamazoo, Michigan, decision in 1874 by the Michigan Supreme Court, which recognized that high schools may be financed from tax monies collected for public education, has been considered as establishing the legal status of public secondary education. Consequently, the free and universal high school became prevalent after 1890. It had a comprehensive course of study and was the avenue to academic and vocational advancement.

Voluntary activity in education has always been a hallmark in America. The National Education Association, founded in 1857, organized several inquiries for the improvement of educational content and administration—for example, the reports of the Committee of Ten on Secondary School Studies (1893) and the Committee of Fifteen on Elementary Subjects (1895). Moreover, education was aided by regional accrediting bodies, such as the New England Association of Colleges and Preparatory Schools (1885), the Association of Colleges and Preparatory Schools of Middle States and Maryland (1892), and comparable associations in the North Central area (1894) and the South (1895).

A contributory factor to the changes in elementary and secondary education was the growth of the teacher education movement. Normal schools were being upgraded and universities were introducing courses in education. By the end of the century, American teachers were becoming increasingly aware of the importance of professional status.

The private schools were also developing during this period. Among such institutions were the Howe, Maryland, Military Academy (1884); Groton (1884), Hotchkiss (1892), and George (1893), famous independent college preparatory schools; and the Gilman Country School, Baltimore (1897). But the greatest growth was shown by the Catholic schools. At the Third Plenary Council in 1884 in Baltimore, the Roman Catholic bishops laid down firmly the principle of a parochial school in each parish and ordered all Catholics to send their children to these schools. The financial problems involved in maintaining a separate school system led some Catholics to make arrangements, as at Poughkeepsie, New York (1873–99), and at Faribault and Stillwater, Minnesota (1891–93), to share facilities and teachers with the public schools, but these were discontinued after much ecclesiastical and lay criticism.

At the end of the century, the organization of the public school system in America was virtually complete, from the elementary school through the university. At the same time, there was evident a parallel organization of independent schools, religious and secular, to meet specialized needs and desires.

CHAPTER II

The Twentieth Century

Prelude to the Present Era, 1900–45

For at least two decades after 1900, there was a vast increase in population, due to natural reasons and to immigration. From 1900 to 1945 the nation participated in two world wars and emerged as an international power, but with a sense of responsibility for contributing to peace. Economically, the country experienced a depression in the 1930's, but recovered its industrial and commercial potential. Social movements of benefit to children, women, and labor came into being.

The elementary school enrollment increased considerably during the first four decades of the century, as did the number of schools and teachers and the size of the educational budgets. Apart from providing adequate facilities, the authorities in the larger cities had to meet the challenge of immigrant children who were to be taught the English language and the American traditions. Special programs were instituted, and these aided in the adjustment of such pupils. Another important problem was the tendency for children to leave school early in order to work. However, child labor laws and the enforcement of the compulsory school attendance laws tended to keep children in school. By 1940, the number of working children had dropped to a minor figure.

Generally, the kindergarten became an integral part of most public school systems, and private kindergartens were also popular with parents. The nursery school movement, however, did not penetrate deeply into public education. The first public nursery school dated from 1919, but this type of education did not gain much ground and most nursery schools were under private auspices. With the advent of the depression, however, the federal government opened nursery schools in line with its welfare program, and during World War II several large cities organized day nurseries to serve the needs of working mothers.

The principles underlying the preschool program were those of freedom of expression, learning through activity, creative work, informal atmosphere, and all-around development of the child. These ideas, generally as expressed in the writings of John Dewey, William H. Kilpatrick, and their followers, began to find their way into the public school system. To some extent, the experiments carried on in the public schools of Gary, Indiana, and Winnetka, Illinois, during the second and third decades were inspired by progressivist ideas.

The subjects studied in the elementary school around 1900 generally covered the three R's, spelling, geography, history, drawing, music, and manual and domestic arts. New developments in society, psychology, and educational theory brought about modifications in the organization and curriculum of the primary school. About 1910, the six-year elementary and the three-year junior high school began to develop. During the late 1920's and the 1930's, the flexible learning program known as the Activity Method was adopted in many areas. Instead of definite subjects allotted to particular times in the daily program, the schools offered large blocks of interrelated knowledge, the acquisition of which was planned cooperatively and informally by teachers and pupils. At about the same time, there arose criticism of these procedures as being unsystematic, inconsequential, inefficient, and destructive of the traditional values of the curriculum. Led by Professor William C. Bagley of Teachers College, Columbia University, this movement was called Essentialism and furnished many of the arguments of the more recent faultfinders.

Intelligence, achievement, prognostic, and diagnostic tests were devised by psychologists and educators to put education on a scientific basis. The training of elementary school teachers began to include child psychology and development. The parent-teacher association, a typical feature of American education in the present century, was organized to bring home and school together.

The application of child psychology, the principle of learning chiefly through direct experience, and the concern with the personality of the individual child were more characteristic of 1945 than of 1900. Memorization fell into disuse because of the prevalent feeling that it contributed very little to understanding. Some educators, not having read John Dewey very closely, made radical changes in curriculum in his name. Accordingly, in 1938, at the time that the Essentialist viewpoint was promulgated, the philosopher issued his *Experience and Education,* in which he warned that the older educational approaches should not be overlooked. Ten years later the child-centered methods, promoted by the Progressive Education Association were still strong, to judge from the principles expressed by the Educational Policies Commission: continuous child growth and development; behavior is learned, not inherited; security and adventure stimulate learning and growth; the uniqueness of each individual; learning is valuable to the extent that it is lived by the child; simultaneous learning; permanent learning through the example of teachers. "Since children learn what they live, the good school is a place where life is as good in quality as the community can devise and provide." [1]

The public high school underwent a phenomenal growth. From 1880 to 1890, and again from 1890 to 1900, there was more than a doubling of enrollment but only a 50 per cent increase in adolescent population. Even more remarkable, between 1900 and 1940 the 13–18 age range rose by about 40 per cent, whereas the high school attendance went up about 1100 per cent. Even though there was a drop in the 1940's, owing to the lower birth rate in the depression era, the figure for 1950 stood at 1000 per cent above that of 1900. Among the many reasons for the transformation of the high school into a mass educational institution was the development of the feeling that it was the American road to culture. The high school broadened its objective of preparation for college to include vocational fitness. By mid-century, most people believed that a fundamental education for American society required, at the very least, a high school education.

The junior high school, which originated about 1910 in Berkeley and Los Angeles, California, and in Columbus, Ohio, came about as a result of the recognition that the upper elementary grades often repeated the content of earlier grades and that the onset of adolescence required a different type of school organization. New courses were made possible in the junior high school—for instance, general science, general language, and general shopwork.

The Report of the Committee of Ten on Secondary School Studies

---

[1] Educational Policies Commission, *Education for All American Children* (Washington, D.C.: National Education Association, 1948), pp. 7–8.

(1893), which laid the groundwork for the popularization of the high school, stated the principle that "the secondary schools of the United States, taken as a whole, do not exist for the purpose of preparing boys and girls for college," but that "their main function is to prepare for the duties of life" [2] those young people who can profit by secondary education and whose parents can afford to support them while at school. Accordingly, the committee recommended a fourfold program for pupils of varying interests and needs: Classical (Latin, Greek, and a modern language), Latin-Scientific (Latin and a modern language), Modern Languages (French and German), and English (including one ancient or modern foreign language). Among the other subjects were English, history, mathematics, and science. Since the modern foreign languages and the English courses of study were labeled by the committee as "distinctly inferior to the other two," [3] they were evidently intended for the pupil not going on to college. Although the report stressed Latin and mathematics and did not give enough attention to manual training, drawing, and music, it turned out to be influential.

The Committee on College Entrance Requirements (1899) recognized the principle of electives in high school and favored a six-year high school beginning with the seventh grade. The National Education Association, which commissioned these and later reports, was not the only organization concerned with the high school curriculum. The American Mathematical Association (1923), the American Classical League (1924), and the Modern Language Association (1929) issued detailed and careful reports. The Modern Language Association revealed that only a small percentage of pupils study a foreign language for more than two years, and it recommended the practicable objective of the acquisition of a basic reading knowledge. While this suggestion proved to be controversial, the report did stimulate the improvement of foreign language teaching.

The report of the Commission on the Reorganization of Secondary Education (1918), also appointed by the National Education Association, formulated a significant and influential set of objec-

---

[2] Report of the Committee of Ten on Secondary School Studies, U.S. Bureau of Education, Bulletin No. 205 (Washington, D.C.: Government Printing Office, 1893), p. 51.
[3] Ibid., p. 48.

tives, frequently called the Cardinal Principles of Secondary Education or simply the Seven Cardinal Principles: (1) health, (2) command of fundamental processes (the three R's, oral and written expression), (3) worthy use of leisure (music, art, literature, drama, and social intercourse), (4) ethical character, (5) worthy home membership, (6) citizenship, and (7) vocational efficiency. This report proved to be an important stage in the development of the high school.

The federal government contributed to the high school curriculum through the Smith-Hughes Act (1917), which furnished annual federal grants to the states for promoting vocational education in high schools and for the training of teachers and supervisors in agriculture, home economics, trade, and industrial fields. This action was followed by similar laws: the George-Reed Act (1929), the George-Ellzey Act (1934), and the George-Deen Act (1936). During the depression, the U.S. government also enabled high school pupils, along with college students, to remain in school through the Federal Emergency Relief Administration (1934) and the National Youth Administration (1935).

The U.S. Office of Education, which sponsored a National Survey of Secondary Education (1933), reported its findings in 27 studies, pointing out suggestions for the "democratization of secondary education" through the provision of special vocational curriculums. A more limited geographical survey, the Regents Inquiry into the Character and Cost of Public Education in New York State (1938), was also studied with care by school authorities.

The *Evaluative Criteria* of the Cooperative Study of Secondary School Standards (1938), was the contribution by a group formed by the regional accrediting organizations (such as the Middle States Association of Colleges and Secondary Schools) to appraise the curriculum, instruction, and administration of high schools. This set of criteria has helped secondary schools in diagnosing their difficulties and improving their standards.

Another private organization, the American Youth Commission, which was created by the American Council on Education, issued in 1940 a report *What the High Schools Ought to Teach*, urging that the school should be adjusted to the needs of all pupils. Specifically, this document stressed the values of reading, current social studies, and work experience as general education; it depreciated the importance of the traditional subjects, especially foreign languages. Along the same lines, the report *Education for All American Youth* (1944), by the Educational Policies Commission of the National Education Association, emphasized the needs of the pupils who were not academically inclined. These and other statements paved the way for the Life Adjustment Education movement in the years following World War II.

The famous Eight-Year Study, sponsored by the Progressive Education Association, involved 1475 students matched in ability and background and enrolled in thirty public and private schools all over the country. The results, published in 1941, indicated that the students from the Progressive high schools were superior to those of traditional schools not only in the arts and in extracurricular activities, but also in scholastic grades and in academic honors. The Progressives' conclusion that the traditional subjects were not really necessary for college was challenged by educators who did not regard the study as conclusive.

Also relevant is the junior college, which is considered by some educators as secondary, particularly when compared to the European secondary school. Education for the thirteenth and fourteenth years of a student's course was proposed in the mid-nineteenth century. However, the first public junior college, at Joliet, Illinois, dates from 1902. By 1945, there were almost 600 junior colleges, public and private, most of them in California and Texas. The junior college offered a partially collegiate, terminal education where full college facilities were not available.

Private secular and parochial schools expanded during 1900–45. A comparison of public and private school enrollments indicated that from 1927 to 1947 the number of public elementary school pupils rose by 14 per cent, compared with a corresponding increase of 9.7 per cent in private school pupils. The 44.5 per cent rise in the total of public high school students, however, was below the rate of increase (76.6 per cent) of private students.[4] To a large extent, no doubt, the growth of the private school attendance stemmed from the bulging enrollments in the Catholic parochial schools. In fact, all private schools were encouraged by the deci-

---

[4] Marion B. Smith, "A Comparison of the Growth of School Enrollments in Public and Non-public Schools of the United States, 1927–28 to 1947–48," *Journal of Educational Sociology*, Vol. 25 (May, 1952), p. 499.

sions of the U.S. Supreme Court in the Nebraska and Oregon cases, which upheld the Constitutional right of private and parochial schools to exist (see pages 25–26).

Between 1889 and 1940, the enrollment in private college preparatory schools increased by almost 500 per cent, from 94,931 to 457,768.[5] Apart from such schools as St. Paul's, which operated on a traditional curricular pattern, there were also Progressive schools such as the Horace Mann, Lincoln, Dalton, Ethical Culture, Little Red Schoolhouse, and Walden schools. Sixteen of the thirty schools involved in the Eight-Year Study were private Progressive high schools. In addition, there were the country day schools, the first of which was the Gilman Country School of Baltimore (1897). The cultural advantage of a country environment in proximity to a large city appealed to a number of educators and parents.

The religious schools, too, gave evidence of growth. In 1952, there existed some 3000 Protestant day schools with a total enrollment of about 190,000 pupils, an increase of 61 per cent since 1937.[6] The Christian Reformed (Calvinist) group started a movement for parent-supported day schools at about the turn of the century to teach the various subjects from the Christian viewpoint. These schools provided "a family tutor system conducted on a communal basis."[7] In 1918, there were 10,401 pupils in the Christian Schools and in 1949 the figure went up to 23,970, well over 100 per cent more.[8] Other Protestant groups, such as the Lutherans, the Episcopalians, and the Seventh Day Adventists, also maintained religious day schools which paralleled the public school system.

The Jewish day school movement, originating in colonial times, developed with interruptions during the nineteenth century and was revived by the end of the century. By 1944, there were 45 Jewish day schools with 9000 pupils. The greatest expansion of this movement was after World War II.[9]

---

[5] Chamberlain, op. cit., p. 50.

[6] National Council of the Churches of Christ in America, Information Service, May 3, 1952.

[7] Mark Fakkema, "The History of Privately-Controlled American Education," in Course of Study for Christian Schools (Chicago: National Union of Christian Schools, 1947), p. 377.

[8] Christian School Annual (Grand Rapids, Mich.: National Union of Christian Schools, 1949), p. 53.

[9] Joseph Kaminetsky, "The Hebrew Day School Movement," School and Society, Vol. 82 (October 1, 1955), p. 105.

In 1951–52, the Catholic enrollment was about 90 per cent of the entire non-public school attendance.[10] Both the Catholic elementary and the high schools grew at a rapid rate. The number of high schools rose from 263 in 1901, to 1552 in 1920, and to 2111 in 1947. The percentages of increase during 1920–47 were 36 for the high schools and 259.8 for the pupils.[11] The registration in Catholic elementary schools, while it did not grow at this rate, was well over two million by 1945.

A factor in the development of private schools was the favorable attitude of the U.S. Supreme Court in several decisions. The first of these involved the right of a private religious school to teach subjects without interference by the state of Nebraska, which prohibited in 1919 instruction of any subject in a foreign language at any public or private school, as well as the teaching of a foreign language in any grade below the ninth. The following year, a teacher in the Zion Parochial School, conducted by the Zion Evangelical Lutheran Congregation, taught Bible stories in German to a ten-year-old. The Nebraska Supreme Court ruled against such instruction, but in 1923, the U.S. Supreme Court reversed this decision by a vote of seven to two. The majority opinion, written by Justice James C. McReynolds, upheld the right of a teacher to teach and the right of parents to engage him to teach their children under the provisions of the Fourteenth Amendment. "Mere knowledge of the German language cannot reasonably be regarded as harmful." [12] Justice McReynolds also pointed out that, since the Nebraska court's decision distinguished between a modern and an ancient language, "the legislature has attempted materially to interfere with the calling of modern language teachers, with the opportunities of pupils to acquire knowledge, and with the power of parents to control the education of their own." The Supreme Court stressed that "the power of the state to compel attendance at some school and to make reasonable regulations for all schools, including a requirement that they shall give instruction in English, is not questioned."

[10] U.S. Office of Education, "Statistics of State School Systems: Organization, Staff, Pupils, and Finances: 1951–52," in *Biennial Survey of Education in the United States* (Washington, D.C.: Government Printing Office, 1955), p. 23.

[11] Sister Mary Janet, *Catholic Secondary Education: A National Survey* (Washington, D.C.: National Catholic Welfare Conference, 1949), pp. 11–13.

[12] All quotations are from the decision *Meyer v. Nebraska*, 262 U.S. 390 (1923).

The next decision, the Oregon case, affected the parochial school more directly and drew upon the precedent of the Nebraska case. In November, 1922, Oregon passed a law requiring all children aged eight to sixteen, with few exceptions, to be sent to a public school. Two corporations operating private schools, the Society of Sisters of the Holy Names of Jesus and Mary, and the Hill Military Academy, obtained from the U.S. District Court temporary injunctions to keep the law from going into effect. The state appealed to the U.S. Supreme Court, which handed down a unanimous decision in 1925 declaring the law unconstitutional. The Court stressed that the Sisters' schools and the military school (a venture conducted for profit) offered the same instruction as did the public schools, except for the addition of the Catholic teachings and military training respectively. It defended the right of the corporations, under the Fourteenth Amendment, to protect their "business and property" from the "unwarranted compulsion" by the state. The Court stated that the Oregon law "unreasonably interferes with the liberty of parents and guardians to direct the upbringing and education of children under their control." [13] Moreover, the Constitution "excludes any general power of the state to standardize its children by forcing them to accept instruction from public teachers only. The child is not the mere creature of the state; those who nurture him and direct his destiny have the right, coupled with the high duty, to recognize and prepare him for additional obligations." This decision defends the right of religious schools, as well as that of a private secular school, to exist under the protection of the Constitution. Some writers have referred to the Oregon decision as the Magna Carta of the parochial school of all denominations.

Still another case involving instruction in a private religious school against a background growing out of World War I tensions, was that of *Farrington v. Tokushige,* which was decided by the U.S. Supreme Court in 1927. In order to promote the Americanism of the pupils, the territorial legislature of Hawaii passed legislation in 1920, 1923, and 1925 forbidding the operation of foreign language schools and the teaching of foreign languages. In 1925, the Department of Public Instruction promulgated a set of rules limiting attendance at the foreign language schools to pupils who were in

---

[13] *Pierce v. Society of Sisters,* 268 U.S. 510 (1925).

attendance at public or private schools, or who had completed the eighth grade, or who were over fourteen years old. It also named the textbooks to be read in the primary grades of the foreign language schools. At that time Hawaii had a total of 163 schools, 147 of which were Japanese, nine Korean, and seven Chinese. Originating in 1896, these schools were private and had an enrollment of about 20,000 children, nearly all of whom attended the foreign language schools after school hours.

The U.S. Supreme Court decided that the territorial law was unconstitutional because "it would deprive parents of fair opportunity to procure for their children instruction which they think important and we cannot say is harmful. The Japanese parent has the right to direct the education of his own child without restrictions. . . ." [14] The Court cited the Nebraska and Oregon cases and pointed out that the Constitution protects the rights of the inhabitant of a territory from infringement by a federal authority under the Fifth Amendment as it protects a resident of a state from the deprivation of his rights under the Fourteenth Amendment. After the decision, the Hawaii legislature gave up its effort to exercise special control over the foreign language schools. Because of the religious nature of the schools, this decision also seems to give protection to parochial schools against unreasonable interference and control by governmental authorities.

The last of the four Supreme Court decisions affecting parochial schools during this period involved litigation in Louisiana, where the state legislature had voted in 1928 to furnish publicly purchased textbooks without cost to children attending schools in the state. Since the law did not specify public schools, the State Board of Education felt that it was legal to provide free textbooks to children in private and parochial schools. Such an interpretation led to a suit by taxpayers who claimed that the law, "supplying school books to the school children of the state," could not be applied for a private purpose. They cited the Fourteenth Amendment and Article IV of the Constitution for support. The U.S. Supreme Court cited the opinion of the Louisiana Supreme Court in rejecting the allegation that the provision of textbooks would help religious or sectarian schools:

[14] *Farrington v. Tokushige*, 273 U.S. 284 (1927).

The schools . . . are not the beneficiaries of these appropriations. . . . The school children and the state alone are the beneficiaries. It is also true that the sectarian schools, which some of the children attend, instruct their pupils in religion, and books are used for that purpose, but one may search diligently the acts, though without result, in an effort to find anything to the effect that it is the purpose of the state to furnish religious books for the use of such children. . . . What the statutes contemplate is that the same books that are furnished children attending public schools shall be furnished children attending private schools. This is the only practical way of interpreting and executing the statutes, and this is what the state board of education is doing. Among these books, naturally, none is to be expected, adapted to religious instruction.[15]

The U.S. Supreme Court concluded that under the Louisiana law "the taxing power of the state is exerted for a public purpose. The legislation does not segregate private schools, or their pupils, as its beneficiaries or attempt to interfere with any matters of exclusively private concern. Its interest is education, broadly; its method, comprehensive. Individual interests are aided only as the common interest is safeguarded." In this decision, the child benefit theory, which was to play a future role in Supreme Court adjudication, was emphasized.

The Recent Past, 1945–63

After 1945, the consciousness of the commitment of the American people to world organization, welfare, and peace shaped the policies of education to a larger extent than it did previously. More opportunities were available to teachers and administrators to travel and to learn other cultures at first hand, and thereby to enrich and broaden the content in the elementary and high schools. There were other forces at work as well. The movement for federal aid to education in order to equalize opportunity all over the nation gained ground, but the achievement was on paper and in oratory, rather than in the halls of Congress. A signal victory for the cause of democracy in education was won, however, when the U.S. Supreme Court in 1954 and again in 1955 declared that separate school facilities for the white and the Negro races were unconstitutional.

A cooperative study involving the federal government and pri-

---

[15] All quotations are from the decision, *Cochran v. Louisiana State Board of Education*, 281 U.S. 370 (1930).

vate educational societies issued in 1953 a statement of objectives for elementary education. According to this document, the desirable and realizable goals of the elementary school are physical development, health, and body care; individual social and emotional development; ethical behavior, standards, and values; good social relations; understanding of the social environment; understanding of the physical environment; esthetic development; acquisition of the skills of communication; and knowledge of quantitative relationships. Specifically, the report stressed "the need for skill in reading, writing, arithmetic, science, spelling, speaking, problem-solving, geography, history, language, civics, health, and all the other fundamental knowledges, skills and competences." [16] Evidently, while considering the adjustment of the individual, the educational leaders felt that subject matter was basic; yet, it seemed to many that the knowledge goals of American elementary education were not being achieved. The forces of dissatisfaction included such books as Rudolf Flesch's *Why Johnny Can't Read* (1955), the Council for Basic Education (1956), and a host of critics, among them Professor Arthur E. Bestor and Vice Admiral Hyman G. Rickover. Their criticism, which echoed the Essentialism of the prewar period, was directed at the activity program which was declared to be the cause of the poor results in knowledge of the fundamentals.

Since World War II, there has prevailed a serious shortage of qualified teachers, as well as an inadequacy of school buildings and teaching materials. There was an apparent inability—or perhaps unwillingness—on the part of the American people to exert themselves to their fullest ability toward the establishment of a first-class system of public schools. Although teacher salaries were raised after the wave of teacher strikes, the competition with salaries in business, industry, and government was such that teachers were attracted to greener fields. Some changes were made in elementary education, such as the growing emphasis on mathematics, science, and modern foreign languages, especially when the spectacular Soviet successes in space seemed to affect the content of all education. By 1963, however, many people were still dissatisfied with the accomplishments of the public elementary school.

---

[16] Nolan C. Kearney, *Elementary School Objectives: A Report Prepared for the Mid-Century Committee on Outcomes in Elementary Education* (New York: Russell Sage Foundation, 1953), pp. 121–22.

The controversy regarding the relations of church, state, and school was featured by litigation on the local, state, and federal levels. Among the results were several U.S. Supreme Court decisions: the Everson case (1947) authorizing free state bus transportation to parochial school pupils; the McCollum (1948) and Zorach (1952) cases involving the release of pupils for religious education outside the public school; and the Regents Prayer case (1962) invalidating a state-composed, nonsectarian prayer in the public schools.

The criticism leveled at the public elementary school was also directed at the high school. The public and scholars criticized the content, procedures, and results of secondary education in the U.S., with unfavorable contrasts, sometimes unfairly, with the products of European (especially Soviet) secondary schools. The American high school, it is only fair to say, was beset with difficulties in relation to teachers and finances. This was no excuse, but it helped explain part of the problem. Defenders of the American public high school pointed up the fact that it was a universal school and much unlike the selective secondary school of Europe.

A part of the conflict regarding the high school was derived from disagreement as to theory and values. The Life Adjustment school of thought was in the ascendancy after World War II. In 1947, the U.S. Office of Education set up a Commission on Life Adjustment Education for Youth. The underlying principle stated that, since most young people do not go on to college, it is necessary to emphasize in the curriculum the areas of the practical arts, health and physical fitness, home and family life, and civic competence as the basis of any program for the needs of American youth. Some educators believed that the Life Adjustment idea, while democratic in intent and application, was not helpful for the student with ability. Some were actually disturbed by the progress of the movement for the core curriculum which tied several courses together and obliterated subject-matter boundaries and which seemed to them to water down content. There was also much displeasure at the prevalence of the elective principle, the presence of fraternities and sororities, the preoccupation with extracurricular (cocurricular) activities, and other aspects of high school life and work which were regarded as distracting from solid subject-matter study.

Some changes were brought about in the 1950's, especially after the National Defense Education Act of 1958 made possible the improvement of teacher training in the sciences, mathematics, and modern foreign languages. The clamor that arose concerning the apparent neglect of the other basic subjects in the high school curriculum led the U.S. Office of Education to organize its Project English in 1961 and Project Social Studies in 1962.

Another important movement was the rise of concern for the education of the gifted and academically talented pupils. The Educational Policies Commission of the National Education Association issued in 1950 a report *Education of the Gifted,* pointing up the fact a democratic ideal in education requires for its fulfillment the best possible scholastic service to the academically capable students. Subsequently, studies and projects on aiding the able were undertaken by various educational groups. Among the recent developments were programs of acceleration, such as the Advanced Placement Program, and the multiplication of state and private scholarships to enable academically qualified graduates of the high schools to go to college.

Of great interest were the activities of Dr. James Bryant Conant, former president of Harvard University, who has been engaged since the late 1950's in making studies of the American high school (1959), the junior high school (1960), the "slums and suburbs" (1961), and the teacher education institutions (1963). Dr. Conant's report on the high school included 21 recommendations for improvement. In his conclusion, however, he underscored the point that "American secondary education can be made satisfactory without any radical changes in the basic pattern . . . only . . . if the citizens in many localities display sufficient interest in their schools and are willing to support them." [17]

Both elementary and secondary education in the early 1960's were characterized by new trends, developments, and procedures: televised teaching, automated or programmed learning materials, team teaching, and so forth. It is much too soon to assess their value or to predict their possible impact on education in America.

Both the public schools and the private institutions have been enjoying a boom in attendance since 1945. The estimated enrollment for 1962–63, according to the U.S. Office of Education, was

---

[17] James B. Conant, *The American High School Today: A First Report to Interested Citizens* (New York: McGraw-Hill, Inc., 1959), p. 96.

35,000,000 for the kindergarten through grade eight, and 11,700,-
000 for grades nine through twelve. These figures, which are combined for public and nonpublic schools, represent a rise of about
two million over the total for 1961–62. The enrollment increase is
for the eighteenth consecutive year.

The private schools have been participating in the new movements and have been troubled by the same problems as the public
schools. Because many of the private schools do not have extensive
incomes and have not been able to raise their teachers' salaries often
or high enough, they have tended to lose able teachers to the public
school systems which have improved salaries and teaching conditions. This problem is especially pressing in the Catholic parochial
school system. Since the number of religious vocations (teaching
nuns and brothers) has not kept pace with the rising population,
and because of rising educational costs and the difficulty of com-
peting with the public schools for lay teachers, there developed a
serious shortage of qualified teachers in the Catholic schools. When
classes were enlarged in an effort to do something about this problem, parents began withdrawing children and sending them to public schools with more favorable teacher-pupil ratios. All these
tendencies have prompted some Catholic educational leaders to propose the discontinuance of some grades in the elementary schools.

The other denominational schools increased in number and registration. Both Protestant and Jewish day schools, as well as private
secular schools, faced problems of costs, teacher shortages, and the
like. Some aid toward the purchase of equipment for the teaching
of science, mathematics, and modern foreign languages was available under the loan provisions of the National Defense Education
Act of 1958, but most Protestant schools refused to take advantage
of the federal law because of their commitment to a strict interpretation of the doctrine of separation of church and state.

Regardless of the difficulties and problems, the private schools
have been continuing their work. Typical of this attitude is a Lutheran comment on the insufficiency of trained teachers of their
faith: "The marvel of it is that congregations go right ahead in
opening new schools and classrooms in the face of this situation." [18]

---

[18] *Know Your Synod's Work* (St. Louis, Mo.: Lutheran Church—Missouri
Synod, 1958), p. 46.

CHAPTER III

Organization of Public Education

The major characteristics of public education in the United States are the absence of a centralized national authority, such as a ministry of education; the existence of fifty state school systems, in accordance with the Constitutionally derived right for each state to control the educational work within its borders; the freedom for all children, youth, and adults to attend public schools and colleges, by Constitutional right, without regard to race, color, or creed; a single educational ladder whereby pupils proceed from one level to the next higher one; administration and control of the public schools by secular authority only; and the enforcement of compulsory attendance laws in all states.

According to the American viewpoint on education, each child and youth, including those who are handicapped in any way, are to be given an opportunity to learn fundamental knowledges and skills so that they can lead a satisfying and satisfactory life of value to themselves, their community, and their nation. In practice, this means that children are taught reading, writing, and arithmetic, since a literate citizenry, as the founding fathers of the United States have stated, is a necessity for a truly democratic government. Moreover, all children learn the historical development of the country and the nature of its ideals and of the democratic process, so that they will be properly equipped to live their lives as intelligent and conscientious citizens. Further, they are given the basic preparation for earning a livelihood and supporting a family. Many young persons, in fact, learn a trade or vocation so that they can work gainfully immediately after completing school.

The American school seeks to bring about the development of the well-rounded individual who can further his latent abilities to their utmost and who can apply noble ideals and ethical purposes in contemplating a decision toward action. It is the function of the public school—and usually of the private school—to help each boy and girl to develop to the limit of his abilities, interests, and

objectives. Unlike foreign countries, the accent is not on the preparation of a select group of leaders and scholars, but rather on the development of every citizen as far as he can go. For those who have intellectual gifts and interests, there are many opportunities and incentives toward scholarship.

The Federal Government

Since the Constitution contains no direct reference to education, education in the United States is basically a function of the several states. The broadness of some Constitutional expressions and the doctrine of implied powers, however, have prompted the federal government to undertake various kinds of educational activities, from the beginnings of the new republic to the present time. In addition, the government controls the District of Columbia and is responsible for carrying on public education there. By Congressional legislation, Guam, Puerto Rico, Samoa, and the Virgin Islands are able to administer their educational systems as the states do.

Congressional legislation has been the source of much federal activity in education for the past century and a half. Since it is not possible to give here a detailed analysis of all the important steps in this direction, only a few illustrations will be cited. In 1865, Congress set up a Bureau for the Relief of Freedmen and Refugees (Freedmen's Bureau), to furnish educational and welfare facilities for the former Negro slaves. In 1950 and again in 1956, Congress authorized funds for the construction of school buildings on federal property and for the maintenance of schools in areas affected by federal defense activities. Moreover, decisions by federal courts exert an influence on public schools whenever a Constitutional question is involved, such as in race relations and in church-state relationships.

The U.S. Office of Education, now in the Department of Health, Education, and Welfare, is the governmental agency which is authorized to gather and publish statistics and other information relative to the American school system, in order to promote the cause of education all over the country. This function has been carried on by this agency since it was established in 1867. However, as Congress passed laws for the distribution of funds for particular educational purposes, such as vocational education under the Smith-Hughes Act of 1917, the Office was charged with the duty of distributing the money. Furthermore, a law in 1896 instructed the Office to pay attention to the dissemination of information on technical and industrial education, compulsory attendance, and foreign school systems. In accordance with the Congressional mandate, the Office has conducted conferences, sponsored research projects by its own staff and by others, and has issued a variety of publications in every conceivable form. A very recent study (about seven hundred pages long) is an encyclopedic survey of the ministries of education of 70 countries.[1] Of special value is the *Biennial Survey of Education in the United States,* which provides current and historical statistics and other information on city and state school systems, higher education, and high school offerings and enrollments. The four-volume *Education Directory* is likewise very useful, inasmuch as it supplies basic information about the personnel on all levels of education—the federal government and the states, the counties and cities, higher education, and the education associations.

The direction of the Office of Education is under the U.S. Commissioner of Education, who is appointed by the President and who has traditionally been a person who has been professionally active in some branch of education. The Commissioner reports to the Secretary of Health, Education, and Welfare, and he also acts as an adviser on education to various government officials. He supervises the work of three associate commissioners and a large staff of educators, administrators, and research workers who are organized into three bureaus: Education Assistance Programs, Educational Research and Development, and International Education. On the administrative side, there are staffs for administrative management (personnel, organization, budget), legislative services, and publications services.

One important function of recent date deals with international educational relations. Apart from the publication of reports on foreign school systems and problems, which the Office has been doing almost from its inception, the Commissioner and his staff have become increasingly involved, since the end of World War II, in

---

[1] Kathryn G. Heath, *Ministries of Education: Their Functions and Organization,* U.S. Office of Education Bulletin 1961, No. 1 (Washington, D.C.: Government Printing Office, 1962).

teacher exchanges with other countries, participation in the conferences of UNESCO and the International Bureau of Education in Geneva, the recruitment of personnel for technical and other educational projects overseas, and other international functions.

The federal government is also active in education through the work of its executive departments and agencies. Thus, the Department of Agriculture aids the school lunch program and assists in providing out-of-school rural education programs. The Department of Defense conducts the U.S. Military Academy at West Point, the U.S. Naval Academy at Annapolis, the U.S. Air Force Academy in Colorado, various service schools (Air University, Army War College), and schools for dependent children of military and civilian personnel who are serving abroad. The Department of the Interior is in charge of education in the Indian reservations, and it aids in safety education and in training in fishery science and wildlife management. The Department of State conducts training programs in the Foreign Service Institute and administers the international exchange of personnel in fields other than teaching below university level. The Department of the Treasury operates the U.S. Coast Guard Academy and several training schools and directs the school savings program of U.S. Bonds. The Department of Justice deals with the educational programs in federal prisons and with citizenship education for persons preparing for naturalization in public schools. The Department of Commerce operates the U.S. Merchant Marine Academy at Kings Point, New York, and organizes civil aviation education programs. The Department of Labor concerns itself with the standards of apprenticeship training and with research on the training and skills of women. Among the agencies with educational functions are the Atomic Energy Commission, the Public Health Service, the Smithsonian Institution, the Library of Congress, the National Science Foundation, and the Veterans' Administration.

It is obvious that the U.S. government is deeply committed to various types of educational work and is doing much to promote education for the growth and development of its citizens. Nevertheless, there is fear on the part of many citizens and educators as to the possible assumption of direct or indirect control over some phase of education by the federal authorities. It is this viewpoint which seems to motivate some of the opposition to federal financial grants to education.

State School Systems

The existence of fifty distinct state systems of education is considered a benefit because it would discourage the misuse of education by a centralized dictatorial power. On the other hand, one can also note the lack of a uniform national standard of education, with the result that there are many weak links in the American educational system. In any event, the state organization of education is important because it is the way by which the schools are controlled.

As a general rule, a state school system is under the control of a policy-making body usually known as the state board of education. Created by the state legislature, the board consists of members who may be elected directly by the people or by the legislature, or, as in most instances, appointed by the governor. Although there is a wide range in the number of members of state school boards, the average is about ten. The term of office may vary from two years to life membership.

Since the state board of education is not a body with professional qualifications as a rule, it is necessary to have the work of administration done by persons who are qualified by knowledge, training, and experience. The highest professional executive of the state school system is the state superintendent or commissioner. He is the chief of the state department of education, which consists of a staff of educational experts. The superintendent of public instruction and the department work together to put into effect the policies laid down by the state board of education. A common method of choosing a state superintendent is by direct election by the people, but in some states he is appointed by the governor or by the state board of education. While the elective office is usually a political one, occasionally the voters may be motivated by educational attitudes. For instance, in the November, 1962, election in California, the electorate, after a long and hard-fought campaign, chose an educational conservative over a liberal in accordance with the public sentiment which was critical of Progressive education.

The state superintendent is often required to have professional qualifications—graduate education and experience as a teacher and

as a school administrator. Obviously, there are no uniform requirements. The chief state school officer may serve from one to six
years, but most officials have a term of from three to four years. In
some states, the superintendent may be in office for an indefinite
length of time, presumably because his efficiency has been recognized by the state government.

The superintendent and his staff, which is organized on the basis
of scholastic level, subject matter, and other educational considerations, are concerned with a variety of matters: the supervision of
the distribution of state funds to the public schools; the regulation
of county and town school systems which are administered by local
boards of education; the setting up of minimum standards for a
course of study for elementary and high schools; the certification
of teachers and administrators; the chartering and accreditation of
schools and colleges; the recommendation of textbooks; the plan-
ning of research projects for study by staff members or others; the
provision of advisory services to local school boards; and other activities, depending upon the state. The New York State Department
of Education administers a unique statewide system of tests (Regents Examinations) of achievement for high school students, issues
professional licenses, and performs other functions of an educational and cultural nature.

Since, under the U.S. Constitution, education is a function of the
several states, all schools—public and private—come under the
power of the state authority. The compulsory attendance law requires that the children be sent to a school, but any child who comes
within the purview of this law must attend a school which is recognized by the state department of education. If there are serious shortcomings in the school, the state may force it to close. With regard
to religious schools, the authority of the state does not extend to
any control over the religious portion of the curriculum, since the
free exercise of religion is guaranteed under the First and Fourteenth Amendments to the U.S. Constitution.

Whenever there is a conflict between the state law and the U.S.
Constitution, it is the latter which prevails. An example of this
principle occurred in 1954 and 1955 when the U.S. Supreme Court
decided that the racial segregation practices in the public elementary and secondary schools were contrary to the doctrine of "equal
protection of the laws" for all citizens as required by the Fourteenth

Amendment. This decision has been accepted, at least on a token basis, by all but three states (1963). A struggle has been going on in Virginia, however, where an attempt was made for a time to interpose the power of the state between the schools and the federal government. In this instance, the principle of ultimate state authority in educational affairs was insisted upon by those who wished to perpetuate segregation.

The state administration of public education is composed of smaller units: the school district (most common), the town or township, and the county. On a geographical basis, the local school district system is most popular in the Middle West, Far West, and parts of the South; the town or township system, in ten states, six of them in New England; and the county system, in twelve states, most of them in the South.

A township is larger than a town but smaller than a county. A township school system may be centralized under a single school board or may consist of several independent school districts. The town school system, as in New England, may be made up of a single geographical unit of villages, suburbs, and a small urban center; or it may consist of a combination of towns constituting a union school district. In effect, a town school district resembles the county school system.

The county school district is under the direction of a county board of education, which may be elected or appointed. It operates the public schools through a professional superintendent who, in most states, is elected directly by the people of the county as a member of a political party. The county superintendent is the local representative of the state school authority and, in this capacity, is involved in the disbursement of funds, certification of teachers, the interpretation of school law, the supervision of the work of the schools, and the promotion of rural education. Depending upon the size and economic status of the county, the superintendent may have a small staff or may be the sole educational functionary except for principals.

The number of local school districts has been estimated by the U.S. Office of Education at about 40,000. In recent years, the number of such districts has tended to be decreased by processes of consolidation. The local school board or board of education directs the public educational system of the district. The members of the board, who are laymen for the most part, are usually elected, although they may be appointed by the mayor, as in New York City. As a rule, the board consists of nine members who represent various interests in the community, and the average period of service is about seven years. The local school board members are expected to have some educational background, a cooperative attitude, a knowledge of community resources and problems, and a definite interest in children and in the various aspects of education. As can well be understood, not all school boards exhibit these qualities, and some may be motivated more by political, religious, economic, or other interests than by the belief in furnishing the best education to the children of the people. In some instances, members of boards may be incompetent, irresponsible, or even dishonest. In general, however, school boards try to be as conscientious as possible in the performance of their duties.

A local board of education is usually charged with the responsibility of the formation of general school policies, selection of the superintendent and other key officials, the raising of funds for schools through the levying of taxes, the adoption of an annual budget and the disbursement of the funds, the selection of school sites, the provision of school buildings and teaching equipment, and other functions which vary from district to district. The members generally do not receive a salary for their services, although their expenses are covered by the budget.

Because of the diversity of practices in the local school districts, one might expect some unusual situations. A unique type of school organization exists in the state of Delaware, where there are no intermediate units of school administration. All the schools of this state are controlled directly by the state board of education.

One practice in the selection of school boards that appears to be peculiar to large city districts with diversified religious, racial, and ethnic groups within the population is the balancing of the boards with representatives of the various elements. As an example, the case of the board of education of New York City might be cited. Here, for many years, the custom has been for the mayor to select three Protestants, three Catholics, and three Jews for membership on the board. These men and women represented at the same time particular boroughs and economic interests, as well as ethnic groups such as the Irish and Italian. In recent years, a Negro, usually a

Protestant, has been appointed to the board. Perhaps, before too long, the large Puerto Rican population of New York City may have a representative on the board of education. While this practice seems to be politically wise and to take into account the needs of minorities, it has been questioned seriously.

In the matter of finances, the school boards have the legal power of levying taxes for school revenues. This seems to be the common practice in the smaller districts. In the metropolitan areas, however, the school budget is part of the total city expenditure. One of the controversial issues in school finance is whether the school board should be financially dependent or independent.

The highest professional official of the local public school system is the superintendent of schools, who is concerned with all aspects of public education. He carries out the policies of the school board and deals with his staff, the teaching personnel, the parents and children, and the general public. The superintendent is customarily chosen on the basis of his higher education, professional training, teaching and administrative experience, standing within the educational profession, ability to deal with the public, and other factors. It is possible in some communities for religion, race, politics, or other educationally extrinsic factors to play an important role in the selection of a superintendent. However, those communities which have had unhappy experiences with a chief school executive appointed in this manner have tried to liberate themselves from this tradition.

A large city school system has a complex school organization. The superintendent has a staff of associate and assistant superintendents who are in charge of particular levels, such as high schools, or of specific services, such as evaluation or personnel. In New York City, there are also district superintendents who supervise a limited geographical area. The superintendents' staffs include specialists in every curriculum field and in each type of administrative and organizational service, such as social studies and evening schools. New York City and other large cities also have a Board of Examiners which administers tests to prospective teachers, supervisors, and administrators, as well as to those in service who are seeking a promotion.

Elementary schools are under the direction of a principal or a teacher-in-charge, according to the number of pupils. The principal of a large elementary school may be aided by one or more assistant principals. A large high school has a principal, assistant principals, and chairmen of subject-matter departments.

The tendency in recent years has been for school superintendents to present higher qualifications for their posts, especially with regard to the depth of preparation in an academic subject. Criticism of public education is one reason that has prompted school boards to demand of their superintendents more than a mere accumulation of credits in courses in administration. The boards also demand a certain degree of scholarship in the superintendents' academic backgrounds. Another current trend is the conception of the position of the superintendent as one of educational expertness and statesmanship instead of mere management. Some of the leading specialists in the preparation of school administrators have also been active in founding a new course of study on a body of educational theory.

The superintendency of a city system carries a great deal of public and professional prestige. Some superintendents, such as Lawrence G. Derthick of Chattanooga, Tennessee, have been called to the U.S. Commissionership of Education, although the general professional opinion of the latter position has not been very high. In fact, one educator, Samuel M. Brownell, resigned his position as U.S. Commissioner and became superintendent of schools in Detroit. One superintendent, Herold C. Hunt of Chicago, for example, became professor of education at Harvard University. Still another instance of recognition is the case of Novice G. Fawcett, superintendent of schools of Columbus, Ohio, who was chosen president of the Ohio State University. Not infrequently, city superintendents of schools are selected to be deans of colleges of education. Thus, John H. Fischer of Baltimore became dean of Teachers College, Columbia University, before being named as president of that institution.

Many functions are exercised, directly or indirectly, by the superintendent of schools: the financial management of the school system, the statement and interpretation of educational aims and objectives, the administration and supervision of personnel, the establishment of courses of study, the provision of information in line with the desirable practices of public relations, educational leadership within the profession and the community, and the coordination of all aspects and services of public education. There is a fixed tenure, which is not the same in all communities, and at the end of the term the superintendent may or may not be re-elected.

Preschool Education

After the previous survey of the administration and organization of the American public school system, it is appropriate to examine its component parts. This system is described as an educational ladder leading from the preschool to the graduate school, or from the doll house to the doctorate. Opportunities are available for virtually all who are able and who wish to climb high.

The bottom of the ladder is the nursery school, which was introduced into the United States from England shortly after World War I. The nursery school serves the need of very young children between the ages of eighteen months and four years. It supplements the early training in the home by promoting the physical, social, emotional, and mental needs of the developing child. The program, which may last from two years to six or seven years, includes indoor and outdoor play with paints, crayons, blocks, and clay; group games; rhythmic activities in music and dance; stories and discussions; food, rest, and sleep; the inculcation of good health habits; and the daily health examination. The nursery schools are often under the supervision of state departments of education, which also establish standards for the certification of nursery school teachers. The operation of a nursery school is a matter of expense, and many public school systems have not been eager to spend part of their limited budget for a form of education which is comparatively new and which has not been recognized to be as necessary as the kindergarten. In spite of the view by some educators that all children can profit from the nursery school experience, there are others who feel that it is in the best interests of most children to have them raised at home during their early years of development.

The kindergarten was introduced into the United States from Germany shortly after the mid-nineteenth century. The "garden of children" provides educational experiences to children between the ages of four and six. The chief function of the kindergarten is the promotion of the children's physical growth and welfare, their ability to work alone and in groups, and their readiness for the three R's of the first grade of the elementary school. As in the nursery school, the program is flexible and informal. Among the child's experiences are work, play, rest periods, music, dance, and story enjoyment. The child usually widens his vocabulary, improves his speech habits, begins to be aware of numbers, and gets ready to learn how to read. Through the achievement of the goals of the kindergarten it is possible for many children to adjust themselves with ease and speed to the elementary school.

The kindergarten, while not compulsory, is becoming more widely accepted by the public. During the 1950's, according to the U.S. Office of Education, the percentage of five-year-old children in the kindergarten rose from about 25 to 50 per cent. In some communities where kindergarten facilities are lacking, a number of five-year-olds will be found in the first grade. Consequently, at the close of the 1950's, nearly two-thirds of the children in the five-year-old age group were either in kindergarten or in elementary school.

Elementary Education

The elementary school was traditionally eight years in length. During the current century, the trend for a six-year elementary school has been prevalent in many parts of the country. In an eight-year school, grades one to three are called primary; grades four to six, intermediate; and the last two grades, advanced. The general objectives of elementary education are the development of knowledge and skills in the basic areas of learning, together with the entire growth of the child along intellectual, physical, social, ethical, and aesthetic lines. At the same time, the elementary school program contributes materially to the awareness of the child of his responsibilities and privileges as a future citizen in a democratic society. While the elementary school is also dedicated to the development of a moral and spiritual consciousness on the part of the pupil, it is not officially concerned with the inculcation of religious, especially denominational, values. Instead, in many schools the children become imbued with a patriotic outlook which may take on a spiritual quality.

Those who have paid attention to the work of the elementary schools are aware of two different basic approaches to subject matter and to teaching. The traditional way favors direct and systematic instruction by the teacher of the subjects which have been in the curriculum for a long period of time. These subjects have been the three R's, geography, history, drawing, music, and a few others. The teacher made use of drill of fundamentals at periodic intervals and exercised a firm type of discipline. Pupils were given homework assignments every day and were examined often. If they were successful in their classwork and tests, they were promoted to the next grade; if not, they repeated the work until they mastered it. Such ideas and practices are, by and large, characteristic of the Essentialist school of thought, which prevailed in the United States until the 1920's, when a widespread attack began to be made on them as destructive of interest, initiative, and individual differences.

The opposing school of thought was the Progressive, which originated to a large extent in the doctrines of John Dewey and William H. Kilpatrick. Progressive educators emphasized freedom for the teacher and pupil, flexibility in the course of study, a broader attitude as to what constitutes achievement and promotion, frequent experimentation, the use of the activity method, and an informal but self-controlling discipline. This approach became more popular in the middle decades of the present century. Many teachers follow a procedure which is compounded of both approaches.

Because the modern elementary school seems to reflect to a large degree the ideas of Progressive education, it would be well to examine them at greater length. Modern educational theory looks upon the school as a form of society where pupils learn what they live, rather than as an intellectual factory where the mind is molded. The school exists for the child as an individual and as a cooperative member of a group. Consequently, his interests and needs, as determined by himself and his teacher, and the interests and needs of the children as a whole are of first importance. This means that traditional subject matter and teaching procedures have to be modified. The concept of activity—learning through the use of the hands and the other senses—has replaced in many schools the practices which encourage passivity on the part of the pupil. Instead of fixed subjects and rigid time schedules, the Progressives have substituted projects which involve learning through the method of research and discussion. The research might lead the pupil to the class, school, or public library, to observations outside the school, to the administration of a questionnaire, and to other practices which take him away from the reliance upon the traditional textbook.

The Progressive school of thought believes in the incidental learning of factual data and the frequent consultation of reference works. This is in contrast to the usual image of the old-fashioned school, where all pupils memorized the same material out of identical textbooks. The newer method, say the Progressives, encourages more critical thinking, enriched learning, better understanding, and more lasting retention. The pupil not only learns content but he also learns how to attack a problem and how to evaluate the information he uncovers.

The status of the teacher is different in a Progressive school. No longer is he standing above the pupil; he is working with him. He is more of a friend and guide than a supervisor who determines his future scholastic progress. When he evaluates the pupil, it is in terms of his abilities and interests, not in accordance with fixed, external standards of achievement.

One of the outcomes of this attitude has been the introduction of a functional emphasis in the curriculum. Since the major concern of the child lies in the present and in the environment closest to himself, a great deal of educational content is related to these interests. Thus, social studies took the place of history, geography, and civics in many schools. On a theoretical level, no doubt, the interrelationship of subject matter is a very helpful procedure. The tendency, however, has been to stress current developments and problems and to underplay systematic history and geography. Not that these were ignored, but the Progressive educators felt that the past should be functional to the present. In other words, history might be mainly presented as a prelude to an important current issue. In a similar way, the systematic study of arithmetic by means of logically sequential steps is not regarded by Progressives to be as significant as the learning through the activity of real life situations, such as selling in the classroom store. The way to learn is through psychological experiencing, rather than through any logical sequence, since the young child can accomplish more, in terms of his development, by the former approach. It is by far easier to interest or motivate the child through what is concrete and real to him. Immediate values and results are considered by Progressives to be more crucial than deferred values.

For some time since the 1930's the Progressive ideas and procedures gained ground in many parts of the country, particularly after research studies pointed to advantages by the newer methods and approaches. The methods of teaching, the structure of the curriculum, and the organization of the elementary school were in a state of flux.

The changes were not made without resistance, however. The Essentialists, John Dewey himself, other Progressives (such as Professor Boyd H. Bode), and various critics pointed out in varying degrees of opposition the shortcomings, especially the extremist variations, of the Progressive school. Moreover, the changes on the world scene in the late 1950's, together with the increased tempo of criticism of the curriculum and methods (of reading, for example), brought about a reconsideration of the status of the elementary school.

Further, there was the change in the nature of subject matter. New developments in the sciences and in mathematics raised the question of bringing the content of the elementary and secondary school curriculums up to date. Committees of scholars in biology, physics, and mathematics met at various times and made proposals as how to modify the content of mathematics and the sciences. In the 1960's, teachers were taking in-service and college courses that would qualify them to teach the new subject matter.

The field of modern foreign languages, which had been a rare subject in elementary education, began to receive serious attention in 1953, after the pioneering conference convoked by the U.S. Office of Education. The common languages that were taught from the primary grades onward in an increasing number of schools were French and Spanish, although others, even Russian and Chinese, made their appearance in some schools. What some educators feared was that public school systems would suffer from the bandwagon effect—that is, the desire to do what others were doing. There was pressure in many communities to keep up with the times by modernizing the curriculum. Moreover, some educators doubted whether there would be any lasting effect, especially in conversational facility, if the higher schools did not continue the foreign language program with the same intensity and enthusiasm.

Secondary Education

The American secondary school, from one point of view, might be considered to be of nine years' duration—the junior high school (grades seven through nine), the senior high school (grades ten through twelve), and the junior college (grades thirteen and fourteen). Although all educators will not agree on this (many arguing for the higher educational status of the junior college), the fact remains that the total secondary school corresponds approximately to the time and content of the standard secondary school in European countries. Since comparisons have often been made between secondary education in Europe and in the United States, it is useful to be aware of this correspondence. Another fact of significance is the nonselective nature of the high school, because there are no examination barriers, as there are in Europe, to attend a school of secondary education. Only a small number of specialized high schools require an examination. It has been estimated that almost nine out of every ten American boys and girls of high school age are undergoing instruction, and the percentage may even go higher. Such a figure is unique in the world.

The fundamental objective of the high school is the provision of a balanced program of general education, so that future college students will have a solid foundation for higher study and the others will have the basic knowledge and general skills to enable them to live a satisfying life as intelligent and informed citizens in a democracy. Recent estimates indicate that more than 35 per cent of American young people are studying in a college or university, whereas in 1910 only about four per cent of the youth were in college. This would seem to indicate that, while most high-school students do not go to higher education, a very significant percentage of young people, more than any other country, carry on their studies beyond the high school. The important fact is not merely the numbers, but the opportunities that young Americans have to advance their education, and thereby their intellectual, economic, and social status in a flexible society. Some of their motivation and impetus, at least, is traceable to the high school.

The customary pattern of secondary education in America is that of the comprehensive high school, which includes in a single institution various programs of study for pupils with different abilities, interests, and ambitions. On the other hand, there are secondary institutions for smaller segments of the adolescent population—for example, the vocational high schools or the science high schools. The noncomprehensive school is found in the larger city systems as a rule. The specialized academic, scientific, or cultural high schools require an entrance examination and, to this extent, depart from the custom of the nonselective nature of American secondary education. Among the specialized high schools of a nonvocational nature are the Central High School of Philadelphia, the High School of Music and Art and the Bronx High School of Science in New York City, and the Cass Technical High School in Detroit. Moreover, there are vocational high schools of every type and description in the very large cities, with those in New York City being highly specialized (for example, automotive trades, textiles, and so forth). Such vocational high schools may be operated in cooperation with a corresponding industry and may have highly expensive equipment. Through a comprehensive high school for the vast majority of American adolescents and through several types of specialized institutions for specific interests, it is clear that secondary education in America makes a definite effort to further the democratic ideal of equal educational opportunities for all persons.

There is some difference of opinion among educators and others on the subject of specialized secondary schools. Since one important value of the comprehensive high school is that it brings together under one roof students of various interests and enables them to intermingle in a natural way, there are some who feel that a specialized high school tends to isolate, perhaps even segregate, some students from the main stream of adolescence in the community. The argument is also raised that students in a special academic or technical school may get a feeling that they constitute an elite. Furthermore, students in a vocational high school might develop an awareness of inferiority. In some ways, this controversy is reminiscent of the long-standing debate of homogeneous-versus-heterogeneous grouping in the schools, and there appears to be a tendency toward grouping of pupils of similar abilities in a single classroom to facilitate instruction. It is not likely that the special classes or special schools have been organized to create any particular elite, but rather to take into account the wide spectrum of individual differences. For some time special attention has been given to the mentally and physically retarded. In recent years, educators have become convinced that opportunities for the academically able are consistent with the principles of democracy.

The breadth of the curriculum of secondary education often depends on the size, location, and other factors of the community. In general, there are two kinds of curricular organization: a group of required subjects to satisfy the needs of all the pupils, and electives for the benefit of individual interests and needs. This form of organization is found mainly in junior high schools, small high schools, and a few of the larger institutions. The subjects are not organized into distinct curriculums. The other type, found in the large high schools, offers two or three parallel curriculums: the college preparatory, general, and vocational. Only graduates of the first are fully prepared to go on to higher education. The others might be able to supplement their studies and thus become eligible for college. Besides the sequence of required courses, each curriculum makes allowance for electives which are open to all pupils.

There are certain subjects—English, mathematics, science, social studies, and physical education—which are common to high schools all over the nation. The actual time devoted to these varies from state to state. Furthermore, subjects like foreign languages are required in some areas and elective in others. Some states require special subjects of all high-school graduates. In view of the entire range of subjects available in high schools, it is evident that a wide variety of needs and interests is taken into consideration.

A recent study [2] by the U.S. Office of Education sheds some light on the subject matter of secondary education. Examining the pupil programs of 1957–58 in about 800 public high schools all over the country, the government specialists found that the typical pupil's program was broken down as follows: English, 24 per cent; social studies, 13 per cent; science, 12 per cent; foreign language, 10 per cent; business, 10 per cent; home economics, 4 per cent; industrial arts, 3 per cent; physical education, 3 per cent; music, 2 per cent; and art, vocational education, health, and driver education, about 5 per cent. About fifty per cent of all pupils earned 73 per cent of all their high school credits in English, social studies, science, mathe-

---

[2] Edith S. Greer and Richard M. Harbeck, *What High School Pupils Study*, U.S. Office of Education Bulletin 1962, No. 10 (Washington, D.C.: Government Printing Office, 1962).

matics, and foreign language. The typical student in the upper one-third of his class obtained 79 per cent of his credits in the five academic subjects mentioned, whereas the typical student in the lower one-third of his class received 70 per cent of his credits in these fields of study. One of the major findings of this study indicates that many of the pupils possessing academic ability could have pursued heavier programs. Another revelation was that many academically able pupils did little, if any, advanced work in mathematics, science, and foreign language. It is interesting that a small percentage of public high school pupils received credit for driver education: only 7 per cent of the boys and 8 per cent of the girls.

The situation since 1958 has been undergoing some change, to some extent due to the international scene. The secondary courses of study in science and mathematics are being modified, as in the elementary school, in accordance with the new content suggested by scholars in these fields. Methods and materials of instruction are also being improved (through the aid offered by the National Defense Education Act of 1958) in mathematics, science, and foreign languages. The U.S. Office of Education reported in 1959 that high schools increased their offerings in the languages, lengthened the sequences of study, and made improvements in teaching procedures. During 1958–59, there was an increase in the number of schools offering Russian, and this trend continued in subsequent years. High schools began to organize language laboratories to give pupils experience in correct foreign speech.

The new spirit in secondary education seems to indicate some sort of reconsideration of the subject-centered curriculum, which had given way in some areas to the core curriculum. The latter, an attempt to integrate subject matter of related types, became rather popular in professional circles in secondary education. Many high schools were combining American literature and American history into a core subject with units of study broader than in the traditional separate subjects. While this form of instruction seemed to coincide with the aims of education, it was criticized by educators as weakening the constituent elements of subject matter.

Dr. James B. Conant, an observer of American secondary education, did not see the necessity of fundamental changes in the public high school, but he did make some specific suggestions dealing with curriculum and organization. While these are not radically new, they show the way for making the comprehensive high school more effective, both with respect to the average and to the academically able pupil. Many secondary educators have been giving serious consideration to Dr. Conant's views on the American public high school.

Mention should be made of a rapidly developing type of extended secondary school (or basic college)—the community college. This is a type of junior college which is becoming popular in various parts of the country. State officials and educators have become convinced that a two-year college is a necessity in many communities, especially where higher educational facilities are lacking or are too distant for daily travel. Such an institution will broaden the opportunity of young people to advance their educational interests and life ambitions. The ideals of a democratic society are again furthered when a community makes funds available for more advanced education for its young citizens. The extent to which a community college represents secondary or higher education depends upon its faculty, students, library, and course offerings. From an international viewpoint the community college is still on the secondary level, since it is basically a school of general education.

Other Forms of Education

It is a commonplace that much of one's education is obtained outside of school and college. There is no doubt that there are many values inherent in such activities as newspaper and magazine reading, radio listening, television viewing, concert going, museum visiting, and the like. Too many persons, however, carry on such cultural and educational activities in a desultory fashion and their total effect is, consequently, very limited. The U.S. educational system provides systematic study for young people and adults who wish to carry on their education. Public libraries offer many opportunities, including discussion groups and courses, for the educationally ambitious adult. Public school systems usually conduct programs of adult education of all types—academic, vocational, cultural, and recreational. Unfortunately, some localities do not have adequate public library facilities and adult educational offerings. Nor is there evidence that masses of Americans are anxious to take full advantage of whatever facilities may exist in their communities for the advancement of education.

Accreditation

The lack of national control over the public school system does not imply the absence of some kind of control outside the state authority. In the first place, colleges and universities can influence high schools by their policies of admission. The state universities of Michigan and California are authorized to accredit high schools in their respective states, but other institutions in these and other states have also had their effect, since high school graduates seek entrance into colleges and universities in many areas.

An important avenue of control by an outside agency is the practice of accreditation by a regional association of colleges and secondary schools, such as the North Central Association of Colleges and Secondary Schools, which was founded in 1895. The standards set up by these associations are required of all institutions which seek membership. Graduates of member schools are eligible for admission to colleges in the various states within the region, which may not be the case in the absence of accrediting agencies. The regional accrediting associations have provided additional safeguards to those of the state departments of education so that the high school diploma would have a meaning outside the walls of the school. Such an influence makes for a certain degree standardization of some portion of the high school curriculum and of requirements for graduation. This is not to say that there are no problems in secondary education. Neither the state departments of education nor the accrediting associations are adequate in the opinion of those educators who favor the establishment of a national board of education which would set up standards for the entire country. On this subject there was a debate in educational circles in the early 1960's.

Statistics

The 1961–62 report submitted by the U.S. Office of Education [3] (on behalf of the U.S. government) to the twenty-fifth annual International Conference on Public Education, convened in Geneva by UNESCO and the International Bureau, revealed a total enrollment of 45,000,000 in elementary and secondary education from kindergarten through grade twelve. This figure was broken down

---

[3] U.S. Office of Education, *Progress of Public Education in the United States of America: 1961–62* (Washington, D.C.: Government Printing Office, 1962).

as follows: public schools, 38,200,000; private schools, 6,500,000; miscellaneous schools (federal schools for Indians and for children of dependent personnel, and so forth), 300,000. The number of children in public elementary schools (kindergarten through grade eight) was 28,700,000; in private schools, 5,300,000. In public secondary schools (grades nine through twelve), there were 9,500,-000 pupils; in private schools, 1,200,000. The enrollment for 1961–62 showed a total increase of 1,100,000 in elementary and secondary schools, including a rise of 200,000 in the private schools.

This report indicated other interesting data: 89.8 per cent of the population between the ages of 14 and 17 were receiving a high school or higher education; 64.2 per cent of all young persons aged 17 in 1959–60 were graduates of high schools; the revenue receipts for public elementary and secondary schools during 1959–60 was $14,759,007,000—with 56.2 per cent derived from local sources, 39.4 per cent from the states, and 4.4 per cent from the federal government; the total expenditures for public elementary and secondary schools during 1959–60 were $15,613,255,000, including 53.5 per cent for instruction, 17.0 per cent for capital outlay, 6.6 per cent for noninstructional school services, 6.9 per cent for operation of plant, 2.7 per cent for maintenance, 3.4 per cent for administration, 3.1 per cent for interest, 5.8 per cent for fixed charges, and 0.9 per cent for other current expenditures; the per-pupil expenditure for 1961–62 was $515, an increase of $43 over the previous year; and 5.41 per cent of the gross national product was spent for all schools (public and private, elementary through higher education) during 1960–61 as compared to 5.10 during 1959–60.

The estimate by the U.S. Office of Education, released in August, 1962, revealed that during 1962–63, the kindergarten through grade eight enrollment in public and private schools would be 35,000,000, while grades nine through twelve would enroll 11,700,-000. The total increase was expected to reach 1,700,000. The National Education Association issued a report (also in August, 1962) on "Financing the Public Schools, 1960–1970," forecasting that the American people would have to spend about $33,000,000,000 a year by 1970 in order to have a public school system to meet their needs. The additions to the educational budget would be necessary to pay for the rising costs of school building construction and teaching equipment, and for the higher salaries required to retain qualified teachers and administrators.

CHAPTER IV

Organization of Private Education

In this chapter, private schools will be classified under the headings of *independent*—endowed or proprietary; *Catholic*—parochial, diocesan, or owned privately or by a religious order; *Protestant*—day schools conducted by the various denominations; and *Jewish*—day schools operated by synagogues or special groups organized for full-time education.

Independent Schools

A definition of the independent school is hard to give, because such institutions are not uniform. It is possible, however, to identify certain characteristics: freedom from political control, ownership and operation by trustees, nongovernmental support, and nonprofit making (with some exceptions).[1] The great majority of the independent schools are recognized by federal and state authorities as charitable institutions and enjoy a tax-free status.

There are several reasons why parents prefer to pay for an education when they have free schools available. Some feel that the public schools are mainly designed for the average pupils and cannot take care of the needs of those who are above average. Such parents are especially anxious that their children be adequately prepared for college, since about 90 per cent of the graduates of private schools continue in college.[2] Another reason is that some parents are not satisfied with the political influences on some school systems. Still others seek special social or athletic advantages not furnished by public schools. The desire for religious content, which is Constitutionally not permissible in public education, motivates many parents to send their children to parochial schools or to independ-

---

[1] Frank D. Ashburn, "Introduction," in *A Handbook for Independent School Operation,* ed. William Johnson (Princeton, N.J.: D. Van Nostrand Co., Inc. 1961), p. 1.

[2] Clarence E. Lovejoy, *Lovejoy's Prep School Guide* (New York: Harper & Row, Publishers, 1958), p. 1.

ent schools which have religious services and a religious atmosphere. In recent years, a new motive has been added to the founding of independent schools—that of avoiding having one's children attend public schools with Negro pupils. Of course, one must not overlook those parents who want their children to go to a school which contains other children of similar if not identical background in economic and social class and in religious belief. Whether one likes it or not, the factor of snobbishness must also be recognized in any discussion of the private school in American society.

Independent schools may be elementary, secondary, or a combination of both. Their classes are usually smaller than those in the public schools. While the teachers' salaries may not be as high as in public schools in many cases, there are teachers who prefer the independent school because they receive board and room or because they feel more at home in an individualistic institution. Many independent schools require entrance examinations of prospective students. Among these are the Secondary School Admission Tests administered by the Educational Testing Service, an affiliate of the College Entrance Examination Board; the tests prepared by the Educational Records Bureau; and other types of examinations.

The control of an independent school is usually in the hands of a board of trustees or directors, who may be the founders of the institution or who may have been appointed by them or their successors. A church or other organization sponsoring a private school may choose its board. The trustees operate under a charter and are charged with policy making, appointment of headmaster, and general responsibility for the institution.

The headmaster carries out the policies of the board of trustees, administers the school, appoints the teachers, supervises the instruction, works on curriculum problems, deals with the parents, and performs other functions. Some headmasters have won fame as guides to young people, as have some of the teachers of the independent schools.

As in the case of the public schools, it is difficult to say exactly what the curriculum of the average independent school is composed of, but there are certain elements which are common to most schools. In the secondary school, there are four years of English, two or three years of history, four years of one language and additional study of another foreign language, three or four years of mathematics, two or three years of science, and religion or ethics. The curriculum of independent schools is often enriched by special courses, such as Latin American and Far Eastern history, Russian, and Chinese. The extracurricular activities, particularly athletics, play an important role in school life. Whatever else the private schools may aim to do, they pride themselves on the significance of the development of character in all students.

Many private schools are members of a coordinating agency, the National Association of Independent Schools, Boston, Massachusetts. The Association was formed in March, 1962, by a merger of the National Council of Independent Schools and the Independent Schools Education Board. About seven hundred schools in 40 states cooperate, through this organization, to expand and improve their curriculums and facilities, to raise the salaries of their teachers, and to obtain more funds for scholarships to worthy and needy students.

It will be instructive to take note of some of the independent schools. The Choate School, Wallingford, Connecticut, is a boarding school which instructs more than 550 boys between the grades of eight and twelve and helps them prepare for college. Established in 1896, this school is nonsectarian and admits students of all faiths and races. Under an Episcopalian priest as headmaster, Choate has a faculty-student ratio of one to seven and a library of more than 20,000 volumes. The tuition in 1962 was $2800 for boarding students and $1100 for day students. Fourteen scholarships, some of them partial, were available for each of the school's classes. One of the recent developments at this school has been the growth of the study of Russian and the summer trips abroad by faculty and students.

The Northampton School for Girls, Northampton, Massachusetts, founded in 1924, enrolls girls for a college preparatory program covering grades eight to thirteen. It is nonsectarian and open to all faiths and races, and daily chapel attendance is required. The day and the boarding students are almost evenly divided. The total student body, about 180 girls, is instructed on a basis of a faculty-student ratio of one to nine. The annual tuition fee is $2500 (1962) for boarding students. The range of scholarships is from $200 to $1000.

The Columbia Grammar School, New York City, is a coeducational college preparatory school from kindergarten to grade twelve. It is nonsectarian. Founded in 1764, it is open to all races and faiths. It admits more than 350 day pupils at an annual tuition fee of $1000 from grade five onward (1962), and scholarships are offered. The faculty-student ratio is one to ten. Religious classes are taught, but they are not required.

The sampling of schools briefly described in the previous paragraphs may not be representative of all types of independent schools or of independent institutions as a whole. One can see, however, a variation in some important details, such as tuition fee and the size of the library. A high rate of tuition is likely to limit attendance to children of the affluent, with very few exceptions. Consequently, the fears of some that the independent schools may be social class schools can be justified to some extent. So far as the library is concerned, it is odd that some expensive schools possess a comparatively small collection of books. Some schools, which are located in large cities in proximity to a public library, may rely on that facility. At any rate, in modern educational work the library occupies a very important role, all the more so when situated in a residential school in a rural area.

One type of independent school which is not customarily considered in educational writings is the military school for boys, many of which are modeled upon variations of the practices of the U.S. Military Academy (West Point) and are directed by West Point graduates. Such schools offer instruction in the same subjects as the other kinds of independent schools, with the addition, of course, of military training. A well-known example is the Culver Military Academy, Culver, Indiana, which has a student body of more than 800 boarding cadets in grades eight to twelve. The annual fee is $2200 (1962). The military training in this academy emphasizes the cavalry, and cadets must pay extra for training in horsemanship. Among the languages taught at Culver is Russian.

The motivation for attending a military school may be the ambition to be admitted to the U.S. Military Academy, the U.S. Naval Academy, or the U.S. Air Force Academy. In such a school, the cadet obtains the rudiments of military science and learns the habit of obedience to superiors, a quality which is essential in a military career and which is not usually fostered in civilian society. It is the disciplinary feature of the military school which appeals to those parents who are convinced that a firm military regimen will correct the behavioral inadequacy of their boys. As one may well understand, the military schools vary in academic efficiency and in ability to guide their cadets.

Very few books on the educational system in America pay any attention to the development, achievement, and problems of independent schools. Although there are many books and other writings [3] on these schools, most works which describe the American school system either ignore the non-public schools or else they might cover the subject in a few pages. Sometimes, such works will discuss the Progressive private schools only. There are several exceptions, however, which attempt to put the private schools into the context of the American system of education. Thus, one volume on the secondary school devotes two chapters on independent education, one on the private secondary school and the other on the parochial secondary school.[4] By way of contrast, another book of similar scope mentions private education in the historical sketch of the American secondary school, but allots only a little more than two pages out of about 750 to a consideration of the independent school.[5] Even though the authors express appreciation of the private school, they give their readers very few data or analysis.

For the very reason that there has been an apparent neglect in American professional educational circles of the role of the independent school in history and in contemporary society, it is appropriate to present to the readers of this book some basic details and ideas about the non-public schools. Surely, more than three centuries' work of the education of American children and young people, together with the extended effort in current education, should qualify the independent school as a component part of the educational system in the United States.

---

[3] Pauline Anderson, compiler, *A Selected Bibliography of Literature on the Independent School* (Milton, Mass.: Independent Schools Education Board, 1959).

[4] William M. French, *American Secondary Education* (New York: The Odyssey Press, Inc., 1957), Chaps. 11–12.

[5] William M. Alexander and J. Galen Saylor, *Modern Secondary Education: Basic Principles and Practices* (New York: Holt, Rinehart & Winston, Inc., 1959), pp. 695–97.

Catholic Schools

The largest of the school systems under the control of a religious denomination is that of the Roman Catholic Church. This system, which also comprises the largest element of the independent schools, did not develop spontaneously, but rather in response to challenges which have arisen in America since the establishment of the hierarchy late in the eighteenth century. The earliest Catholic schools in America go back to colonial times, but the parish schools seemed to have originated under the inspiration of Archbishop John Carroll of Baltimore not long after the establishment of the new republic. Elsewhere in this book there appears an historical sketch of a portion of Catholic education in the U.S. (see Chapter I). [6] Special attention was given to the development of the parochial school, which enrolls the vast majority of the children in Catholic schools. It is interesting to note that although the regulations laid down by the Third Plenary Council of Baltimore (1884) and by Canon 1379 of the Code of Canon Law (1918) stipulate that bishops open one elementary school at least in every parish, it has been observed that the growth of Catholic schools in the U.S. resulted "more from the private convictions of thousands of individuals than from the coercive force of law." [7]

Despite the common impression that all Catholic pupils are in Catholic schools, it is closer to actual fact to say that only about half of the children of school age attend such schools. Among the reasons for this situation are the lack of sufficient schools, the cost to the parent, the complications of intermarriage, the critical attitude by some parents toward the results achieved, the large size of classes, inadequate teaching materials, and the narrow curriculums. On the other hand, there are parents who are convinced that the moral and spiritual teachings of the Catholic school and the devotion of its teachers by far outweigh any of the shortcomings. Interestingly, in some parts of the country the new Catholic schools

---

[6] For a full history, consult J. A. Burns and Bernard J. Kohlbrenner, *History of Catholic Education in the United States* (New York: Benziger Bros., Inc., 1937). See also Gerard S. Sloyan, "Roman Catholic Religious Education," in *Religious Education: A Comprehensive Survey,* ed. Marvin J. Taylor (Nashville: Abingdon Press, 1960), pp. 402–5.

[7] Sloyan, *op. cit., p.* 402.

rival in modernity those of the public school system, a point which appeals to a certain kind of parent.

The various terms in Catholic education should be differentiated. All Catholic schools are private in the sense that they are not financially supported by the public. However, the parochial or parish school, which is under the direct supervision of the parish priest, is usually considered in Catholic circles to be quasi-public. High schools for pupils of various parishes are diocesan institutions—that is, under the bishop. These are also in the category of a parochial school. The non-parochial schools are regarded as private, since they are owned by religious orders, such as the Jesuits, the Christian Brothers, or the Ursuline Sisters. Despite these distinctions, in actual practice all schools in a diocese are under the direction of the bishop and his educational staff.

The Catholic school is neither a carbon copy of the public school in the neighborhood nor an "all-week Sunday school," where the children are drilled for six hours daily in the catechism by nuns, pray in the church next door, and bear the parish priest's exhortations.[8] On the basis of such an image, anyone might believe that the real objective of Catholic educational work is indoctrination pure and simple. While Catholic education does have a supernatural foundation and seeks to infuse the entire curriculum with Christian values, it is still concerned with the development of young people "as scholars and citizens." [9] This means that the content of the subject matter taught in the Catholic schools must be substantially the same as in the public schools. The difference is that the Catholic courses will modify the content in order to highlight Catholic values. These differences do not alter the fact that the Catholic student is expected to know what all others do when he takes a uniform state examination, as in New York State, or the College Entrance Examination. Perhaps the brief discussion of the Catholic aim in education might be well illustrated with a quotation from a prominent educator: "If the process of education . . . is to fulfill its function of developing the whole person, a principle which has universal approval, the Catholic educator considers the task incompletely performed unless knowledge of God and our duties to Him are in-

[8] Neil G. McCluskey, S.J., *Catholic Viewpoint on Education* (Garden City, N.Y.: Hanover House, 1959), p. 73.

[9] Sloyan, *op.cit.*, p. 406.

cluded in the educational program." [10] It must be recognized that in Catholic education there is no uniformity in the achievement of the program or the accomplishment of the objectives.

Catholic parents and educators are not always satisfied that the intellectual and cultural aspects of education are satisfactory in their schools and colleges. This attitude has been evident, in a large measure, during the past decade, when leaders like Monsignor John Tracy Ellis, the historian, and other scholars have criticized what they term the low level of attainment by Catholics in the scholarly and professional fields. Another difficulty of which Catholic educators are aware is the excessive parochialization of parochial school pupils. For their purposes, they feel, the idea of separate education is best, but they are worried about the possible isolation of large portions of Catholic youth from the rest of the population. As a result, efforts are being made to minimize the separation.

According to Catholic educators, their schools teach the obligation of the pupils toward the various races, political views, and economic levels in society. With reference to religion, of course, the pupils are taught that the Roman Catholic Church is *the* Church of Jesus Christ, and that the members of the other faiths occupy an equal status as fellow citizens. This is not to say that the Catholic school teaches that all religions are equal. On the contrary, the attitude of the necessity "to share the treasure of faith" with non-Catholics is instilled in pupils, without encouraging this practice to "degenerate to the level of proselytism." [11]

Catholic education in the U.S. is organized by archdioceses (under an archbishop) and dioceses (under a bishop). The highest ecclesiastical officer is actually the archbishop or bishop, but because of manifold duties he entrusts the direction of education to an archdiocesan or diocesan superintendent of schools, who corresponds to a state or county superintendent of public instruction. The diocesan superintendent, or secretary for education as he is sometimes called, is a priest (often with the rank of monsignor) who has had special training in professional education in a Catholic or secular college or in both. The superintendent administers and supervises the entire school system of the diocese, and he helps in the coordination of the courses of study and in raising the standards

[10] Sister Mary Janet, S.C., *op. cit.*, p. 9.
[11] Sloyan, *op. cit.*, p. 407.

of education in every respect. In a highly populous diocese, such as Brooklyn, the superintendent will have a staff of priest-educators to assist him. As the educational right-hand man of the bishop, the superintendent is in charge of all parochial and diocesan schools, as well as all schools operated by the religious orders of priests, brothers, and nuns.

The vast majority of Catholic elementary schools and a number of the high schools are parochial; that is, they are financed by the Catholics of a particular parish and are under the direct supervision of the parish priest, who is responsible to his bishop and to the parents. As a general rule, the instruction in the parochial elementary schools is carried on by nuns who are members of religious orders. The parish priest, if qualified, is the principal; otherwise, the school is directed by a nun.

The diocesan department of education, like the state department, has school boards, which are required under the orders of the Third Plenary Council. Although these boards at one time were actively engaged in raising the standards of education, in recent times they have functioned as advisory groups to the bishop and superintendent. The diocesan school board of Pittsburgh consists of twelve priests (including the superintendent, who acts as secretary) under the chairmanship of the bishop. Since all the board members reside in the diocese, they are subordinate to the bishop; but the bishop is interested in the views of the board members, who have had rich and varied educational experience. The annual report by the superintendent includes the enrollment, a description of the new developments, an analysis of problems, and suggestions toward solutions. One superintendent, in submitting his report on behalf of the diocesan school board, expressed the hope that "these suggestions may be useful to Your Excellency in formulating policies which will strengthen the cause and broaden the scope of Catholic education." [12]

Again, as in the state school systems, the superintendent of a large diocese will be aided by supervisors of special fields of instruction, such as music and art. Superintendents, supervisors, and teachers are prepared in Catholic and non-Catholic colleges, teachers' colleges, and universities. They are organized into special asso-

---

[12] The Very Rev. Msgr. John B. McDowell, *Catholic Schools, Doicese of Pittsburgh: Fifty-Sixth Annual Report, 1960–1961* (The Diocese of Pittsburgh), p. 3.

ciations such as the Jesuit Education Association, and these groups are usually constituents of the National Catholic Education Association (founded in 1904) which holds annual conferences, issues publications, and is otherwise active in raising the standards of the Catholic educational profession. The executive secretary of this organization, which is set up in a fashion similar to the National Education Association, is Msgr. Frederick G. Hochwalt, who is concurrently the secretary of the Department of Education of the National Catholic Welfare Conference, the agency of the bishops of the United States. Of great significance toward the improvement of education in the parochial schools was the establishment of the National Sister Formation Conference to raise the level of the spiritual, intellectual, and professional training of the nuns who teach and will teach in the parishes.

With regard to the financial support of Catholic schools, the national survey [13] by the National Catholic Welfare Conference revealed that, in 1947, most secondary schools obtained regular contributions from parents, full support from the parish funds, or a combination from both sources. Other methods were full support by the diocese, a diocese-parish-parent combination, and endowment or charitable funds. The financing of parochial elementary schools may be from parish funds, from tuition fees, or from both. The rate of tuition differs from parish to parish. In one parish, in the late 1950's, the actual tuition charge was $10 per family per year without regard to the number of children in attendance. To this were added a book rental charge of $5 and miscellaneous fees of $2.25, so that each family paid $17.25 for the first child and $7.25 for each of their other children in parochial school. Families which are not able to pay may have their children taught in the school without tuition charge.[14] From a number of reports, it is evident that the financing of the parochial school is regarded as a serious problem by Catholic educators and parents.

As already mentioned, most of the Catholic elementary and high schools are parochial and diocesan. There are also schools maintained and operated by religious orders, where tuition fees may be charged. The Country Day School of the Sacred Heart, Newton,

---

[13] Sister Mary Janet, *op. cit.*, p. 21.
[14] Joseph H. Fichter, S.J., *Parochial School: A Sociological Study* (Notre Dame, Ind.: University of Notre Dame Press, 1958), p. 351.

Massachusetts (for girls, preschool through grade twelve and college preparatory), required up to $1800 of its boarders in 1962 and about $700 of the day students. The cost at the LaSalle Military Academy, Oakdale, Long Island, New York, under the direction of the Brothers of the Christian Schools, was $1800 in 1960 for boarding cadets. Some of the urban high schools, such as the Regis High School in New York City, a Jesuit institution, have achieved recognition for high scholastic standards and for the acquisition by the graduates of many scholarships and honors. An archdiocesan institution, Cardinal Hayes High School in New York City, for example, may reach the size of a large public high school. The tuition fee at this school was $5 per month in the mid-1950's.

The Catholic elementary schools offer the same basic curriculum taught in the public schools, with the addition of Catholic values. Their leaders, too, are reorganizing and modifying the content and the methodology in science, mathematics, and other subjects. Experiments are being initiated with team teaching, television, tapes, electronics, and other modern procedures and facilities. Cooperation is taking place between parents and teachers in conferences and in home-school associations.

Among the newer organizational experiments are enrichment of subject matter and ability grouping. These have been going on for several years in the face of opposition by some parents and teachers.[15] As a matter of fact, there has been a sort of tradition in Catholic education to resist the newer methods and theories in education. On the other hand, some educators have felt that unity is necessary in the matter of essentials—on the aims in education and on the viewpoint on the nature and destiny of children, but that with regard to method and other "accidentals" it is possible to have "the most glorious squabbles." [16] A survey by a Catholic educator in the mid-1940's pointed out that diocesan school systems varied in attitude from "extreme conservatism" to a comprehension of and sympathy with the principles of Progressive education. In his conclusion, however, this priest acknowledged that Progressivism is neither totally good nor bad. Its philosophy is "prevailingly unsound and unacceptable," but some of its practices are effective, and Catholic

[15] McDowell, op. cit., pp. 8–24.
[16] William J. McGucken, S.J., The Catholic Way in Education (Milwaukee, Wis.: Bruce Publishing Co., 1934), p. xiii.

educators were urged to consider the practices provided they could be "utterly divorced" from the naturalistic philosophy of Progressive education.[17]

Any discussion of the curriculum in the parochial school must take the religious factor into consideration. Since at the bottom of the Catholic aim and effort in education lies the inculcation of religious ideals and attitudes, it has been felt necessary by the church authorities to produce Catholic textbooks in science, social studies, literature, and certainly religion. At the present time, there are Catholic series of textbooks for practically every school subject to make certain that no undercurrent of materialistic and naturalistic philosophy runs through the instruction in the parochial schools.[18]

According to one Catholic educational expert, the average elementary parochial school teaches formal religion five daily periods of half an hour each. The content of the religion course comprises catechism, doctrine, Bible, and church history. The classes are taught by nuns, priests, and lay teachers. While some schools may stress the teaching of religion more than others, most appear to preserve some sort of balance between the religious and the secular subjects.[19] The schedule of time in the eighth grade of one parochial school indicates that the pupils spent 25 hours a week according to the following breakdown: English, 37.3 per cent; social studies, 16 per cent; arithmetic, 15 per cent; religion, 10 per cent; music, 6.7 per cent; science and health, 5.3 per cent; art, 4 per cent; and recess and miscellaneous, 5.7 per cent. In other words, two and a half hours out of a total of 25 are taken up with the study of religion. The priest-sociologist who made an investigation of this school admitted that the incidental religious activities, such as talks on religious vocations, choir singing, and altar serving, may cut down the time allotted in public schools to shop, sewing, and physical training, but he insisted that these were of an educative nature and were an integral and necessary part of the education of the parochial school pupil.[20]

---

17 The Rev. Laurence J. O'Connell, *Are Catholic Schools Progressive?* (St. Louis, Mo.: B. Herder Book Co., 1946), pp. 155–56.

18 Sister Mary Richardine, B.V.M., "Catholic Elementary Education," in *The Official Guide to Catholic Educational Institutions* (New York: Catholic Directory Co., 1960), p. 27.

19 McCluskey, *op. cit.,* pp. 109–10.

20 Fichter, *op. cit.,* p. 106.

The curriculum of the Catholic high school [21] resembles that of the public high school: mathematics, the sciences, ancient and modern foreign languages, English, social studies, fine arts, practical arts, and physical education. Religion, of course, is present in every Catholic curriculum as a required subject for four years. The teaching of religion in some schools may be quite minimal—as little as thirty minutes per week—although many institutions devote from three to five clock hours each week to this subject. As in the elementary parochial school, additional time is spent on various religious activities which contribute to the realization of the basic objectives of Catholic education. The formal course content covers the study of Catholic doctrine, Bible and church history, apologetics, the liturgy, the Papal Encyclicals, and other sources of Catholic moral and social teachings.

The courses of study in social studies in Catholic secondary schools comprise American, world, ancient, medieval, and modern history, civics, sociology, problems of American education, and other subjects. The foreign languages offered are mainly Latin, Spanish, and French, although a number of schools teach German, Greek, Polish, and Italian. The stress on Latin is understandable because of the close connection between this classical language and the liturgy and literature of the Catholic Church. In fact, in recent decades there has been a trend toward courses in Church Latin, in which pupils read portions of the Church Fathers, the Epistles, and the liturgy in the original. In general, however, the role of Latin in Catholic secondary education may not be as strong today as a quarter of a century ago. The current changes in subject matter, equipment, and methodology are also affecting the curriculum of the Catholic secondary school.

Catholic elementary education in 1960 was marked by an attendance of 4,373,422 in 10,501 schools; secondary education, by 880,369 students in 2392 schools. A total of 108,169 teachers were in the elementary schools: 74,842 sisters, 3652 priests, 625 brothers, and 27,384 female and 1666 male lay teachers. In the secondary schools, there were in all 43,733 instructors: 21,243 sisters,

---

[21] Sister Mary Janet, S.C., *op. cit.*, pp. 65–92. See also Sister Mary Janet, S.C., "Catholic Secondary Schools," in *The Official Guide to Catholic Educational Institutions*, pp. 22–23.

7492 priests, 3875 brothers, and 6030 male and 4793 female lay teachers. Clearly, then, nuns make up close to 75 per cent of the teaching force in the elementary schools and nearly half of all teachers in the high schools. Another fact of interest is that the enrollment in both the elementary and the high schools is almost evenly divided between boys and girls.[22]

The problems affecting Catholic education are many and are highly complicated. Together with public education, the Catholic system suffers from overcrowded schools and classrooms, difficulty in the recruitment and education of teachers, inadequate financial resources, and the like. Specifically, Catholic schools may not always have the variety of offerings which is a characteristic of the public school. They may find it difficult to pay their lay teachers the type of salaries which would keep them from being attracted by the public school salary schedules. Then again, the combination of financial, personnel, curricular, and other factors may create an image in the minds of the parents and the public that the Catholic school is not effective or that it is not doing its share for American education.

Catholic educators, however, appreciate the Catholic school, because they identify several contributions made by it to the welfare of the country:

1. For over a century it trained immigrant children as loyal American citizens.

2. It pursued the principle of racial integration and pointed the way to the desegregation of the public school system.

3. It has tried to supplement the official, secular school system with one based on Christian teachings.

4. It has taught the moral law of God as the basis for personal happiness, civic virtue, patriotism, and international peace.

5. It has recognized and maintained the pluralistic nature of American society.

6. It has created a system of religious education which can serve as an example to Catholics in other countries.

7. It has shown that Catholicism is a firm and reliable basis for training good citizens.

8. It has saved the American taxpayer more than one billion dollars a year by supporting schools for over five million Catholic

---

[22] *Summary of Catholic Education—1960.* Release by the National Catholic Education Association, Washington, D.C.

pupils who would otherwise have had to be educated at public expense in the public schools.[23]

How long the Catholic school system will be able to exist in the world of rapidly mounting costs, limited budgets, and rising pupil populations is a matter for serious thought. In Catholic educational circles, there has developed a difference of opinion regarding the future of their school system. Since the financial difficulties of operation for such a network of schools seem to be insurmountable and any aid from a public source is apparently improbable, some Catholic educators have been suggesting, during the past decade, that the first three or four grades of the parochial school be discontinued. It is obvious to them that the current facilities and teaching staffs are by no means adequate enough to furnish an elementary and secondary education for all Catholic children. At the same time, they feel that the most pressing need of moral and spiritual education, such as provided in a parochial school, is from the age of ten to eighteen. At the present time, less than 25 per cent of the Catholic boys and girls of high school age are in a parochial school. For youngsters who will be deprived, under this plan, of a religious education in a full-time Catholic school, the educators propose that the parochial school set up afternoon classes for them several times a week. Thus far, this solution to the problem of Catholic education has not made much headway beyond the stages of discussion and publication. Many Catholic educators oppose it because of their conviction that the first four years of the child's formal education are more important—from the psychological standpoint— for moral and spiritual education than the later years are. Moreover, it may be too difficult for children to adjust themselves from a secular school atmosphere to a religious one.

Since the plan of a parochial school beginning with the fifth or later year does not appear to be on the way to fulfillment, Catholic educators feel that they must revise the methods of financial support of the parochial schools. One method that is apparently achieving some success is a tax levy upon all parishes for the development of a diocesan school fund. In this way, the wealthier parishes would

---

[23] Rev. James P. Shannon, "The Contribution of Catholic Schools in America," in *The Role of the Independent School in American Democracy* (Milwaukee, Wis.: Marquette University Press, 1956), pp. 91–92.

aid those which are less affluent. One large diocese which levied an assessment of 20 per cent of gross income upon each parish was able to provide a Catholic high school education for every boy and girl in its jurisdiction.[24]

In considering the problem of the financial support of Catholic schools, it would be well to consider that their clientele often represents the lower economic levels and that the people's ability to pay for their children's education is consequently very limited. It is true that the church does not pay salaries and fringe benefits to the sisters and brothers who constitute a very large proportion of the teaching staffs. It should not be overlooked, however, that it takes considerable money for the education of the religious, in order that they might obtain the proper preparation for teaching in the parochial schools. Generally, a large and expensive institution instructs relatively small numbers of future nuns, brothers, and priests. Further, while the religious are engaged in teaching, they must be fed, housed, and clothed, and many must be provided with books and with funds to study for advanced degrees. Accordingly, the hidden costs of parochial education make it more costly than it seems to be at first glance. For this reason, Catholics consider the financial question as a key issue in their parochial school system.[25]

Protestant Schools

The rise of public school systems during the first half of the nineteenth century led to a decline of the virtual monopoly of education by religious groups since the early seventeenth century. Some of the Protestant denominations, such as the Presbyterians and the Methodists, gave up their schools and threw their support to the public schools. Other groups, however, decided to continue and expand their own schools while adopting a positive attitude toward public education. Among the denominations which operate all-day schools are the Quakers, Mennonites, Lutheran Church-Missouri Synod, Episcopal, Calvinist (Christian Reformed), and Seventh-Day Adventists. There also are many private schools which are

---

24 McCluskey, *op. cit.,* pp. 108–9.
25 John E. Wise, S.J., "American Catholic Schools Today," *School and Society,* Vol. 82 (October 1, 1955), pp. 102–3.

affiliated with or related to at least thirty Protestant religious groups, such as the Baptist, Mormon, Methodist, Presbyterian, and Episcopal.

Because of the diversity of the Protestant schools, it is difficult to do justice to their aims in a sentence or two. However, most of the leaders of Protestant full-time weekday schools (which also might be referred to as Protestant parochial schools in the broad sense of the term) agree that religious teaching should be the central theme and focus of the school program every day, rather than a special class. They are concerned with Christian education and specifically with the administration of their schools as evangelistic agencies in which their own children are indoctrinated with the beliefs of their respective churches, thereby contributing to the survival and extension of the churches.[26] The public schools, they feel, are secular and many insist that they remain secular or at least nonsectarian, in accordance with the historic Protestant tradition of separation of church and state.

The motivation for the establishment of parochial schools by one Protestant group may be illustrated by its characterization of the work and objective of the public school as "secular." According to a spokesman for this group, the National Union of Christian Schools, a secular life is "Bible-less, God-less, Christ-less, Atheistic, immoral, lawless, corrupt." [27] On the positive side, another writer states that the proper education "requires a positively Christian school which by its whole atmosphere and through its teaching as such tightens this living relationship between the child and his sovereign God and Father. Arithmetic must so be taught that the fascinating orderliness of numbers reflects the intelligence of the great Creator of all." [28] It will also be useful to cite another expression of the nature of the work of the parochial school from another denomination: "Lutheran schools aim for moral instruction in depth: first of all, by impressing religious convictions; second, by showing how religious belief, to be genuine, must affect all areas of life; third by training their students in the Christian life which they

---

[26] Raymond S. Moore, "Protestant Full-Time Weekday Schools," in Taylor, *op. cit.,* p. 237.

[27] Fakkema, *op. cit.,* p. 375.

[28] Edward Heerema, *"Of Such is the Kingdom,"* (Grand Rapids, Mich.: National Union of Christian Schools, 1950), p. 9.

advocate." [29] Moral education, thorough academic instruction, and training for responsible citizenship constitute the triple objectives of the Lutheran parochial school.

A few examples of Protestant private schools might be briefly described. The Collegiate School, New York City, founded in 1638 and probably the oldest private American secondary school in existence, is affiliated with the (Dutch) Reformed Church. It offers college preparatory and other programs to more than 300 day boys between grades one and twelve. The tuition rate is from $550 to $850 (1958). Saint Albans School, Washington, D.C., founded in 1909 and related to the Episcopal church, is a college preparatory school with grades four to twelve. The 400 boys, most of whom are day pupils, were charged $1900 for board-tuition and from $775 to $840 for tuition in 1958. The Western Christian High School, Hull, Iowa, established in 1919, is a coeducational institution affiliated with the Christian Reformed Church. The school conducts college preparatory, general, and commercial programs for about 350 students. In 1958, the day tuition was $160 and the boarding tuition was $280. Saint Louis Lutheran High School, St. Louis, Missouri, founded in 1946, is a coeducational school with college preparatory, general, commercial, and special programs for about 800 day students. Tuition was $140 in 1958.

The Quaker and the Episcopalian schools are often usually independent of church control. A member institution of the National Union of Christian Schools and similar groups is controlled by parents of the denomination and is known as a parent-society school. The other types are the parochial, the diocesan, and the conference schools, each of which is under the direction of the respective level of church organization.

During 1957–58, the largest enrollments in church-related elementary schools were shown by the Lutheran Church-Missouri Synod (130,124 in 1175 schools), the Seventh-Day Adventists (42,069 in 825 schools), the Christian Reformed (31,874 in 160 schools), the Joint Synod of Wisconsin (21,901 in 208 schools), and Protestant Episcopal (12,028 in 128 schools). On the secondary level, the highest registration figures were recorded by the Prot-

29 Wm. A. Kramer, "Public Service of the Lutheran School," in *Religion, Government, and Education,* eds. William W. Brickman and Stanley Lehrer (New York: Society for the Advancement of Education, 1961), p. 59.

estant Episcopalians (17,900 in 104 schools), the Seventh-Day Adventists (13,380 in 290 schools), the National Association of Christian Schools (7942 in 49 schools), the Lutheran Church-Missouri Synod (7022 in 13 schools), and the Christian Reformed (6664 in 26 schools).[30]

The funds for the various types of Protestant schools are raised by endowments, direct tuition, indirect tuition through pledges to the church, tithes or offerings, and subsidies and donations from the diocese or conference. The financing and operation of the schools is considered in many denominations as "evangelistic or mission projects," and since the teachers have evangelical or missionary functions, often their salaries are subsistence wages, below the level of the public schools in the community. Fear of government control and adherence to the principle of church-state separation now inhibits some parochial schools from accepting government surplus foods or government scholarship programs.[31]

The school system of the Lutheran Church-Missouri Synod maintained in 1961 close to 1300 elementary schools which instructed 150,000 pupils (about one-third of the eligible children) and 20 high schools enrolling nearly 20,000 students. The schools of all Lutheran groups have an enrollment of almost 200,000 elementary and high school pupils, more than ten per cent of whom were non-Lutherans.[32] During the decade 1947–57 elementary school attendance in the Missouri Synod rose by nearly 50,000 and the number of schools increased by 158. Although its schools constituted only 36.4 per cent of all Protestant elementary schools, the Synod had in 1958 "decidedly the largest Protestant school system in America." [33]

The curriculum of the Christian Schools (Christian Reformed) for grades one to nine might be cited as an illustration of what is taught in Protestant parochial education. The *Course of Study for Christian Schools* (1947) starts with the philosophy and general objectives of Christian education and then proceeds to outline, grade by grade, the subjects of Bible Study and Church History, mathematics, reading and the other language arts, social studies,

---

[30] Moore, *op. cit.*, p. 242.
[31] *Ibid.*, pp. 244–45.
[32] Kramer, *op. cit.*, pp. 53, 55.
[33] *Know Your Synod's Work: 1958* (St. Louis, Mo.: Lutheran Church-Missouri Synod, 1958), p. 46.

science, physical education, and fine arts. While the content is substantially the same as in the public schools, this syllabus makes it clear that each subject must be taught in a "God-centered" framework. Thus, "the study of algebra is intended to result in the greater glory of God through the restoration of the child of God toward his intended God-likeness." [34] History, which is "a record of God's revelation in the affairs of the human race," must be taught in such a way that pupils will learn how "to read the handwriting of God in the events of history . . . how the entire course of past events reveals divine direction, control and purpose." [35] In the field of science, the Christian teacher is "to lead the child into the realm of nature—God's nature—where he too may learn to read God's thoughts as he has revealed them in the creatures and the objects of his creation." [36] It must be understood that not all Protestant schools use this approach and that all follow more or less the elementary and secondary school curriculums in their respective states, with the addition of religious content and atmosphere in varying degrees of intensity. Most Protestant schools do not emulate the example of the Lutheran and the Christian Schools in the publication of special textbooks which are infused with religious spirit and values.

The Protestant parochial schools serve their churches and their country by experimenting with new educational ideas and procedures; by providing boarding facilities for children of isolated or broken families; by organizing in one institution all grades from the kindergarten through the twelfth, thereby enabling the school to adjust more readily to the personality of the church and the community; by maintaining, as the Methodists and others do, separate schools for boys and girls, so that education in a formative period can be carried on without the distractions of the opposite sex; by furnishing in some boarding schools, such as those of the Seventh-Day Adventists, daily work experience to balance the intellectual program, thus aiding inculcation of desirable qualities of character as industry, order, and integrity; and, most distinctively, by providing the "freedom to develop religious attitudes of their choosing

---

[34] *Course of Study for Christian Schools, op. cit.,* p. 129.
[35] *Ibid.,* p. 215.
[36] *Ibid.,* p. 288.

and throughout the entire curriculum to indoctrinate their students in the tenets of the parent faith." [37]

According to one Protestant educational specialist, "the Protestant day school will not become a major factor in Protestantism in general." [38] Contributing to this conclusion are the financial effort for expansion, the commitment to the public school, the difficulty of obtaining a sufficient number of teachers who qualify both as educators and as Christians, and the necessary limitation of secondary education to academic schools.

Jewish Schools

Although Jewish education in America takes on a variety of forms, the only school where an intensive and comprehensive religious education is offered is the Jewish day school or *Yeshivah ketanah* (junior academy) as it is often called in the Hebrew language. This type of elementary institution, which combines two programs—Jewish and secular studies—dates from 1731, but the modern period started in 1900 with the founding of the Rabbi Jacob Joseph School in New York City. The *Yeshivah* movement on the secondary level or *Mesivta* (senior academy), as it is sometimes known in the Aramaic language, was inaugurated in 1915 with the establishment (also in New York City) of the Talmudical Academy (now the Yeshiva University High School for Boys).

The aims of the Jewish day schools have been expressed by an educational leader who directs Torah Umesorah, a national society which helps establish and guides such schools, as the leavening of a definitive body of Jewish religious knowledge, observance of Jewish law and custom, preparation for advanced Jewish studies, love of the people and land of Israel (historical and current), and the *"integration* of the best of American culture and Jewish values." [39] Day schools may differ in policy on such matters as coeducation, language of instruction, financing, organization, schedule, relative emphasis to religious and secular studies, and the degree of adherence to religious tradition. Most of them are Orthodox, and they

---

[37] Moore, *op. cit.,* p. 245.

[38] D. Campbell Wyckoff, "The Protestant Day School," *School and Society,* Vol. 82 (October 1, 1955), p. 101.

[39] Joseph Kaminetsky, "Evaluating the Program and Effectiveness of the All-Day Jewish School," *Jewish Education,* Vol. 27 (Winter, 1956–57), p. 42.

teach belief in the Torah (sacred scriptures revealed by God) and adherence to its commandments.

Each school is an independent unit and is free from any control beyond that of its self-perpetuating board of directors, who are mainly concerned with the raising of funds, and its board of education, which sets the policy for the educational program. The two boards, single or in cooperation, appoint the principal, who usually chooses and supervises the teaching staff and works out the details of the course of study. In many schools there are two principals and two teaching staffs, one for the religious and the other for the secular program. The trend in recent years has been for the selection of personnel, especially the principal, capable of functioning in a dual capacity.

The religious course of study includes intensive study of the Bible and commentaries in the original Hebrew, portions of the Talmud in the original Aramaic, Hebrew grammar, prayers, and religious law. Many schools add Hebrew conversation and Jewish history. Music and arts and crafts also appear in some schools. The language of instruction may be Hebrew, Yiddish, or English. The only Jewish language taught is Hebrew, and Aramaic and Yiddish are generally learned by the pupils in an informal and incidental manner. The total time given to religious studies may range from 15 to 25 hours per week. The secular studies are the same as in the public elementary and high schools, but they tend to emphasize the academic. The atmosphere of the day schools is religious, and the pupils pray in school and practice the religious observances. Thus far, no special textbooks have been produced for teaching secular subjects, which are taught as in the public schools and sometimes by Christian teachers. Citizenship and loyalty to the U.S. are inculcated into the pupils.

In 1962, according to a report by Torah Umesorah, there were 274 day schools in 28 states and the District of Columbia. Of these, 116 are located in New York City. Included in the total number of schools are 57 secondary schools, 31 of them in New York City. The pupil population was estimated as 50,000, with 35,000 being taught in the metropolitan New York area.[40] The schools are fi-

---

[40] Torah Umesorah, *Facts and Figures on the Growth of the Hebrew Day School* (unpublished report, 1962), p. 1.

nanced mainly by voluntary contributions and tuition fees, but a few of the Jewish communities also give some small subsidies.

Among the problems facing the Jewish day schools are adequate financing resources; an insufficient supply of properly trained teachers; and the persistence of opposition by some segments of the Jewish community on the ground that the schools undermine the public school system, segregate Jews from the rest of the population, and are contrary to the spirit of what these Jews conceive as Americanism. On the other hand, the unusual development of the Jewish day school movement has given much encouragement and inspiration to those who are concerned with its future progress.

Relation to Public School System

In this chapter, various kinds of private or independent schools have been described and analyzed in more or less detail. The data indicate that the aims and general content of such schools parallels rather closely those of the public school system. The teachers of the private schools are trained in the same institutions as are the public school teachers. There are obvious differences, of course. The private religious schools add religion or seek to permeate all their teaching with spiritual values; but the subject matter that is taught remains essentially the same as that of public education, and the graduates of these schools are given no special entrance examinations to college that are not also given to public school graduates. The private schools are not financed from public sources, but they perform a public function by preparing well-informed young citizens who serve their country and fellow-men in an official or private capacity. At the same time, the state authorities exercise supervision and control over all the private schools within their borders. For all these reasons, it is reasonable to advance the hypothesis that the independent school in the public service, which teaches over ten per cent of the nation's children, and the public school are partners that coexist in the dual American educational system.

CHAPTER V

The Controversy Over Federal Aid
to Public Education

Background of the Issue

Federal aid to public education may be traced to the 1780's at the time of the Congress of the Confederation. All through American history, the national government has given some aid to education and has itself engaged in educational activities. Attempts were made to enact laws for more substantial systematic aid to education in the closing decades of the nineteenth century. Since the end of World War I, there has been an increase in the number of bills for federal aid, and the events of the depression and of World War II convinced many persons of the imperative need for federal assistance to the states in some form or another to bring about an equalization of educational opportunity for the youth of the nation and to raise the standards of national education and culture. Since World War II, Congress has considered a large number of bills, passed some, but failed to enact most of them.[1] The pressure for federal aid is continuing nevertheless.

Federal Aid: Pro

Among the groups for federal aid to public schools are the National Education Association, the American Federation of Labor—Congress of Industrial Organizations, Americans for Democratic Action, the American Council on Education, the American Federation of Teachers, the Council of Chief State School Officers, and other organizations. Many of these issue statements which indicate

---

[1] Helen A. Miller, *Federal Aid for Education: A History of Proposals Which Have Received Consideration by the Congress of the United States (1789–1960)* (Washington, D.C.: Committee on Education and Labor, House of Representatives, Government Printing Office, 1961), pp. 41–72.

a positive attitude toward the idea. From these organizations, as well as from individuals, emerge several arguments: [2]

The national government requires an intelligent, well-informed citizen population if it is to achieve its aims in a democratic way. The welfare of all the people is in danger as long as people in certain sections of the country have not received a basic and adequate education. This situation is especially true in wartime, when the people are more interdependent. In recent decades, there has taken place a great deal of population mobility, and no one section can escape an immigration of persons who may have had an inferior education. Further, the education of the Negro has suffered and is still suffering in some parts of the country, and the resultant migration brings about educational problems in the new areas of settlement. The federal government can bring its resources to bear on the matter of raising the level of education all over the country by helping the states, especially those which find difficulties in properly supporting their schools. The rise of federal taxation has left less funds in individual pockets, and the states and local communities have less to tax. Consequently, it is up to the federal government to correct the deficiency.

The principle of federal aid to education has many historical precedents. During the twentieth century, Congress passed legislation to supply funds for vocational education, for schools in federally affected areas, for school lunches, for aid to high school students during the depression, and for improving instruction in the defense subjects (science, mathematics, and foreign languages) in the elementary and secondary schools. Other laws also aided schools in one way or another. All these acts of Congress have been passed in harmony with the power in the Constitution to "provide for the common defense and the general welfare of the United States" (Article 1, Section 8). As of the present, there has been no challenge of any of these in the U.S. Supreme Court. If "general welfare" covers the Congressional laws of the past which aided education, it

---

[2] Summaries of arguments, pro and con, can be found in Charles A. Quattlebaum, *Federal Aid to Elementary and Secondary Education* (Chicago: Public Administration Service, 1948), pp. 103–44; *Congressional Digest,* Vol. 38 (June–July, 1959), pp. 170–91; Roger A. Freeman, *Taxes for the Schools* (Washington, D.C.: Institute for Social Science Research, 1960), pp. 375–97; and Frank J. Munger and Richard F. Fenno, Jr., *National Politics and Federal Aid to Education* (Syracuse, N.Y.: Syracuse University Press, 1962), pp. 19–75.

is reasonable to suppose that it will likewise cover any future legislation which attempts to raise the nation's standard of living in culture through education.

A general law for aid to education will reduce the glaring inequality of educational opportunity which is derived from the low standards and from the low budgets in some states. It is well-known that the less affluent states, especially in the South, have been making more of an effort than the richer states to give their children an education, since they have been spending greater proportions of their tax revenues for the public schools. The lack of sufficient funds, however, means that the Southern states' exertion to provide an adequate public school system is bound to fall far short of the goal.

Annual grants to the states by the federal government will help promote the equalization of educational opportunity. Such grants, to be disbursed by the U.S. Office of Education, which has had much experience with the allocation of federal funds, will bring about significant changes for the better in economic, political, and social spheres of activity through the promotion of citizenship, economic literacy, and vocational competence.

Proper safeguards in the laws will prevent any possible control of any aspect of education by the government. A century or more of federal aid to education has not resulted in any interference with or control of the institutions which received grants. There have not been recorded any serious complaints of any control in connection with the G.I. Bill of Rights or with the funds granted or lent under the National Defense Education Act of 1958. Naturally, the government has the right to require a financial account to make sure that the states spend the federal funds for the purposes specified in the law. This is a practice which is universally recognized as reasonable and just. The increase of federal aid to the states will so promote the educational effort, efficiency, and expansion all over the country that it may result in a reduction of the direct federal programs of education, some of which have been supervised and administered by officials who have not had adequate professional training and experience. In some cases, they have exercised undesirable controls. Federal aid to the states would put an end to such practices.

Other countries support public education from national funds, and the U.S. is a rare exception in not furnishing aid for general educational purposes. All over the world, education is recognized as a matter of national concern. It is not enough for the federal government merely to urge the states to improve education; it must lend a helpful hand, since it depends on the products of the educational systems of the states. To some extent, the universal example of the national government as a partner in the educational progress may be followed by the U.S. without in any way compromising the Constitutional right of the states to control their own schools.

Federal Aid: Con

Opponents of federal aid to education include the Chamber of Commerce of the U.S., the American Legion, the American Farm Bureau Federation, the Daughters of the American Revolution, the National Association of Manufacturers, and various other organizations. Some of these groups, such as the American Legion and the American Farm Bureau Federation, were in favor of governmental aid in the 1930's and 1940's before shifting their attitude, possibly in response to urging by the Chamber of Commerce. The National School Boards Association, which consists of about 150,000 school board members, adopted a resolution at its annual convention in 1961 in opposition to federal aid. However, a poll of its membership in 1962, while upholding the opposition to general federal support, indicated approval by the majority of the school lunch program, aid to federally affected areas, vocational education, and the National Defense Education Act. Although the National Congress of Parent-Teacher Associations is in favor of federal aid, some of its constituent state organizations (Indiana, for example) have expressed disapproval.

The lack of mention in the U.S. Constitution of "education" or "school" is an indication of the fact that the founding fathers intended that education remain the province of the states rather than of the central government. Indeed, the Tenth Amendment provides that "the powers not delegated to the United States by the Constitution, nor prohibited by it to the States, are reserved to the States respectively, or to the people." Hence, education is a function of the state, the local government, and private initiative. The "general welfare" clause, which is often cited as authority for educational activity by the U.S. government, is interpreted in too sweeping a manner. If the framers of the Constitution had wanted to include education, they would have specified it, as they did other matters. It would be wrong, therefore, for the government to break with the tradition of state, local, and private support for education.

The state and local control of education would be jeopardized by the provision of federal funds to public schools, since some kind of control is inevitable. It will simply not be sound for the government to allocate money to the states without inquiring about the uses to which it has been put. This inquiry might, in a number of cases, have to go beyond mere information as to how much was spent for what purposes. The moment the government appoints itself the judge as to whether or not the funds have been wisely expended, it begins to exercise some control. Under such circumstances, the federal power asserts itself and it must necessarily interfere with the rights of the states to administer and control their own educational affairs.

There is also a danger that the state school systems might become standardized and regimented. Since the states will want their cut from the national pedagogical pie, they would be inclined to make whatever adjustments that would be necessary to qualify for the allocation of federal money. This would mean that the natural development of the state system would be discouraged and that the only type of progress that would be possible would be under the aegis and control of the federal government. The net result would be standardization, regimentation, and centralization. A centralized kind of educational control would be destructive of the democratic nature of the U.S. and its institutions.

There is no real need for federal aid for public education, since virtually all states have been improving their economic and industrial output and potential. In other words, the states can really support their public school system if they only determine to do so. After all, the amount of money which is spent on such luxury items as candy, tobacco, and cosmetics is enormous. Moreover, there is plenty of money for cultural and recreational facilities of a more or less socially approved nature. All the states have to do is to educate their own citizens so that they would want to ensure better schools by paying for them more than they have ever paid before. Further, there has been a wastage of funds, for various reasons, in some states. Only after a state has seriously tried all the possibilities for raising funds within its own confines and has found it impossible to support its schools adequately, then and only then should it apply for assistance to the U.S. government.

It is impossible, and undesirable if possible, to equalize educational opportunity so long as there is no fully centralized and nationalized public school system. The educationally advanced states, under the present system, will continue to forge ahead, while the retarded states will never be able to catch up with them even with federal aid. As with individuals, it is inevitable that the differences in educational quality will remain among the several states. If there is no possibility that there will ever be full equality in education for all the citizens of the U.S., because of the variation in human capacity and motivation, then it becomes a futile gesture to legislate equality by pretending that money will bring about equality of educational opportunity. Moreover, any state which wishes to make its school system the equal to that of a neighboring state should try to attain such an objective by its own efforts. Finally, where racial segregation still exists, federal funds might possibly perpetuate inequality of educational opportunity by strengthening out of proportion the educational facilities of the white race.

Federal aid is likely to destroy the initiative of the state to improve its school system. The state legislature might not want to prepare an adequate school budget and would be inclined to look for largesse from Washington. Instead of depending upon its own resources, which is the traditional American way of doing things, there is every possibility that available federal funds would weaken the will of the states and of the American people to pay fully and thus to control their public schools. It is also important to realize that more money is not necessarily the key toward the advancement of education. A good education cannot be purchased, but can only be secured by an exertion of considerable effort. If the state and local school authorities should discipline themselves to make full and better use of the personnel and facilities already available, and if they see to it that the schools stress subject matter and dispense with frills, then there will be no need for any radical rise in the school budget. Under these conditions, federal aid would surely not be necessary.[3]

The Outlook

The arguments on either side of the issue of federal aid to public education show strengths and weaknesses. The general impression that the great majority of the American people would like to see the federal government render aid to the states derived from the resolutions by labor, educational, religious, and other bodies. More dramatically, toward the end of 1955, at the White House Conference on Education, there was a demonstration of public opinion on the question. In spite of some distrust that the Conference would resolve against federal aid, a majority of more than two to one approved the proposition that the national government should give more aid to the states for education, particularly for the construction of school buildings. There was an almost even division of opinion regarding the provision of federal funds for the operation of local schools, but only a very small group stated its opposition to any form of federal support of education. Congress, however, did not translate this expression of the popular will, even though under official auspices, into any form of legislation. The issue of federal aid to education has become complicated, not only because of the controversial nature of federal aid in general, but also by reason of its association with the issues of religion and race. Not even the support of a popular President, Dwight D. Eisenhower, who shifted his position to approval of aid to school construction, could cause a break in the impasse in Congress. Nor had President John F. Kennedy been able to make a dent of any sort, even when in January, 1962, he revealed that "a massive attack" upon illiteracy must be undertaken to educate eight million "functionally illiterate" adults in the United States. Significantly, the hitherto less controversial area of federal aid to higher education became affected by the religious issue, and Congress rejected in September, 1962, a bill for a federally aided program for college construction and student scholarships. The only type of major federal legislation for education was the National Defense Education Act of 1958, but this was passed for emergency reasons.

---

[3] Roger A. Freeman, *School Needs in the Decade Ahead* (Washington, D.C.: Institute for Social Science Research, 1958), p. xxvii.

In December, 1963, Congress passed a bill providing $1,560,-000,000 for vocational education, schools in areas affected by the national defense, and loan funds for college students. Another significant piece of legislation was the Higher Education Facilities Act of 1963 which furnished $1,200,000,000 in loans and grants to public and private colleges and universities for the construction of buildings to be used in teaching and research. Despite this acceleration of activity by Congress, there was nothing done for the aid of the broader purposes of education.

From all appearances, the likelihood of general federal aid to public education is very slender in the foreseeable future. Most people seem to want it, but they are not prepared to agree to overlook the related issues in order to achieve the realization of federal participation in the support of public education. One of the few possibilities for federal aid would seem to be the growth of a conviction that the survival of the nation in the international society of today depends upon a strong school system.

CHAPTER VI

The Controversy Over the Existence
of the Private Schools

Notwithstanding the long history of private education in the U.S. and its instruction of at least one-tenth of American children and youth, there are individuals and groups questioning the right of the private school to exist. No one has made any attempt to go as far as the voters of Oregon did in 1922 to force all children into the public schools. However, the indifferent or negative attitude on the part of a portion of the profession and the public may become a deterrent in some places to the growth of independent education in the United States.

The criticisms of the private schools mainly concentrate on three points: (1) they are institutions of special privilege for the wealthy few, who are encouraged to retain a snobbish, exclusive, and elitist attitude; (2) they cannot educate as effectively as the public schools do; and (3) they weaken the public school system by attracting many qualified students and by using up public funds which might otherwise have been spent for the benefit of public education. Each of these arguments deserves some analysis.

School for Snobs?

There is little doubt that there are private schools which cater to the snobs, but these seem to be relatively few. There are also schools which will discriminate among applicants for admission on the grounds of religion, race, and economic and social class. Even the exclusive schools, however, have scholarships, and many institutions state that they are open to all races, colors, and creeds. Nor can the private school be distinguished from the public by labeling it a class institution. While this charge may seem to be true of the independent school which charges high tuition fees, it is surely not applicable to the parochial school, which draws its pupils in most cases from the various social and economic strata.

On the other hand, the public high schools in the metropolitan suburbs may be, because of residential restrictions, veritable one-class schools. From the standpoint of the racial question, moreover, it is obvious that the recent campaign in the communities and in the courts to put an end to *de facto* segregation in the urban and suburban public schools is recognition of the fact that even in public education there may be practices which prevent the free intermingling of pupils.

Effectiveness of Private Education

Some tend to question whether the private schools are better than the public schools or if the former are effective at all. It is most difficult to evaluate properly a single school, public or private—especially one in a system in which there is wide variety. Apart from this, reliable comparisons between one school and another, and especially between one system and another, are complicated and at times discouraging processes. Yet, there are some indications which have been derived from several studies.

One of the early studies in depth comparing the scholastic results of graduates of public and private schools revealed that the public school graduates were superior in college work.[1] Similar conclusions were formed by others who compared the later success of the public and the private (parochial and secular) students.[2] The researchers offer various explanations for the difference, but it is probable that the conclusions are no more than tentative. More studies have to be made of various types of schools at different times and in various locations.

It is interesting to glance at the findings of the most recent research study which analyzed the scholastic records of two equal numbers (103) of parochial and public school graduates who had matriculated at the Ball State Teachers College, Muncie, Indiana, each fall from 1952 to 1957. The parochial group was superior in

[1] Leonard V. Koos, *Private and Public Secondary Education: A Comparative Study* (Chicago: University of Chicago Press, 1931).

[2] A brief summary of studies is given in Robert E. Hill, "Scholastic Success of College Freshmen from Parochial and Public Secondary Schools," *School Review*, Vol. 69 (Spring, 1961), p. 60.

scholastic aptitude, especially in linguistic aptitude, possibly because the parochial schools stress verbal skills. When the factor of scholastic aptitude was overlooked, there was no significant difference between both groups in scholastic achievement, "although all differences obtained favored the public school group." [3] When it was controlled, however, the public school group had "a statistically significant superiority" in scholastic achievement. The researcher concluded that, since he did not seek the causes of the results, his judgments must remain "speculative."

The findings of these studies deny the opinion prevalent in certain colleges and universities that the graduate of the independent school is scholastically superior to the public school graduate. This may have been true at one time, but probably is not true any longer. In spite of the criticisms of public education, there have been improvements over the years. The processes of selection for admission to the favored colleges have been made more objective, and the students from lower social groups now have more chances to attend the prestigious schools which attract the affluent and aristocratic alumni from the independent schools. Moreover, once in the university, the graduates of the urban high schools tend to apply themselves with vigor to their studies.

Another type of evidence should be taken into account. In New York State, in recent years, some of the highest ranking winners of the Regents Scholarships have been graduates of Catholic and Jewish parochial schools. A study of the annual lists would reveal the persistence of more graduates from some independent and parochial schools than from others. This would seem to indicate that some schools—whether private or public—achieve better results consistently than do other institutions. In short, some light has been shed on the question of the effectiveness of the private school, but the final word, if any is possible, has not been said.

Weakening of the Public School

The presence of a school which parallels the public school in a community is considered by some to be a threat to the system of public education and perhaps to democracy itself. One type of

---

[3] *Ibid.*, p. 65.

charge is that the independent schools make it difficult for public schools to do their best "by draining off the best parents and students." [4] To the extent that these parents, who are often influential, become involved with private schools, they are unable or unwilling to show an interest in the public schools. There is also an opinion that the Catholic parochial schools, in particular, constitute a danger since the Catholic Church seems intent on obtaining public support, and this support would cut into the funds which would be made available for public education.

The idea of the danger of the private school has been expressed by several leaders in education. Thus, Professor John S. Brubacher of the School of Education of the University of Michigan, a renowned philosopher of education, has repeatedly asserted that the real threat to democracy lies in the fact that the independent school is an impediment to sharing by different groups of the population. Since it withdraws its clientele from the public school, the independent institution either has something which it does not desire to share with the public school or something in the public school which it does not wish to share. In any case, Professor Brubacher sees in the existence of the private school an invitation to "misunderstanding" and perhaps "even misgiving." [5] Nevertheless, he concedes that in a democracy those who are not satisfied with the public school have the right to open the kind of school they want. The U.S. Supreme Court, in fact, has definitely committed the country to a "pluralistic rather than monistic or totalitarian view of public education." [6]

The widely influential educator, Dr. James B. Conant, spoke and wrote often in the early 1950's about the threat to our democratic unity which was inherent in the presence of young Americans in the independent schools instead of in the public high schools. He expressed his regret that the public high schools did not enroll all the boys and girls of a community.[7] The furor which followed this statement implied that this view was revolutionary. As a matter of

---

[4] Ashburn, op. cit., p. 6.

[5] John S. Brubacher, Modern Philosophies of Education, 3rd ed. (New York: McGraw-Hill, Inc., 1962), pp. 142–43.

[6] John S. Brubacher, A History of the Problems of Education (New York: McGraw-Hill, Inc., 1947), p. 567.

[7] James B. Conant, Education and Liberty (Cambridge, Mass.: Harvard University Press, 1953), pp. 81–82.

actual fact, it represented no basically new idea. More than two decades earlier, a well-known professor of education at the University of Chicago had argued that parochial schools would not be consistent "with the best good of an integrated American society." [8] Interestingly, a recent study disclosed that the children of a Catholic elementary parochial school, apart from their religious background, "appear to be immersed in the same socio-cultural milieu" —movies and television—as the children of the public school in the community. To the author of this sociological analysis, it was obvious that the Catholic children's extracurricular interests and activities were more influenced by the home and neighborhood than by the parochial school.[9]

Over-all View

The private schools have their defenders and opponents. No doubt, there is some truth in the various accusations and criticisms of the independent school and of the public school as well. But after all the complaints, one should not forget the more than three centuries of service to the nation which has been rendered by private education. The private schools were the pioneers of American education and then developed alongside the more rapidly growing public school system. As keepers of the heritage of religious education, which has been valued in America from its inception, they have been able to teach what has been officially forbidden to be taught in the public school. Many of the independent schools have been successful examples to public education in experimenting with new ideas and practices. Both the public and the private school have long labored to give America a good educational system. The achievement of the public system is amply, if not lavishly and constantly, recognized. It remains to give due credit to the independent school as an important partner in the formation of a high level of American society, culture, and education.[10]

---

[8] Koos, *op. cit.*, p. 217.

[9] Fichter, *op. cit.*, pp. 442–44.

[10] William W. Brickman, "The Historical Background of the Independent School in the United States," in *The Role of the Independent School in American Democracy* (Milwaukee, Wis.: Marquette University Press, 1956), pp. 80–81.

CHAPTER VII

The Controversy Over Church-State Relations in Education

The issue of what should be the relationship between religion, government, and education has been rather explosive in recent decades, especially since the late 1940's. The war between those who wished and those who opposed public aid to parochial schools was almost alternatingly hot and cold. Other aspects of church-state school relations also turned out to be productive of vigorous, sometimes fierce, debate. A vast amount of literature has been produced on all sides of the issue. In this chapter, an attempt will be made to present the highlights.[1]

Background of the Issue

The American doctrine of separation of church and state reaches back in history to the discussions by the founding fathers of the Constitution and the resultant First Amendment (1791) stipulating that "Congress shall make no law respecting an establishment of religion or prohibiting the free exercise thereof." Through the Fourteenth Amendment (1868), this prohibition was eventually recognized by the courts as binding upon the states. The precise meaning of the term, "establishment of religion," has long been a matter of debate, but the U.S. Supreme Court and other courts have interpreted it, in the words of Thomas Jefferson, as "a wall of separation between church and state." In actual practice, all through American history this famous phrase has been applied by the courts in different ways, apparently not always with consistency.

As a general principle, the "wall of separation" was invoked whenever the problem of public aid to religious schools came up

---

[1] For a multi-faceted introduction to the question, in the U.S. and abroad, see William W. Brickman and Stanley Lehrer, eds. *Religion, Government, and Education* (New York: Society for the Advancement of Education, 1961).

for consideration in the legislatures and the courts. At the same time, the public schools were not usually regarded as an establishment of religion, even if religious teachings and practices were carried on, so long as a nonsectarian atmosphere prevailed. The Catholics regarded such an environment as Protestant and founded, in consequence, their own school system (see Chap. IV). Even if the American attitude is negative toward federal and state support of parochial schools, some subvention was given to schools and colleges under religious auspices from the time of the Northwest Ordinance (1787) until well into the twentieth century.[2] Moreover, as already indicated, U.S. Supreme Court decisions have been favorable toward state provisions for free bus transportation and secular textbooks for children attending parochial schools. Under such conditions, it is not a simple matter to delineate with any exactitude the doctrine of church-state separation in relation to the question of public support of parochial education. Nor is it easy to apply this doctrine to public schools when the Bible has been read, prayers have been recited, and religious customs have been practiced for more than a century.

Also of some pertinence is the persisting tradition in American society that the U.S. is a Christian country. The argument of Daniel Webster that a nonsectarian Christianity was "the law of the land" was upheld in 1844 by the opinion of U.S. Supreme Court Justice Joseph Story that the Christian religion was "part of the common law of the state."[3] In an even more direct form, the idea appeared about half a century later in the opinion of U.S. Supreme Court Justice David J. Brewer that "this is a Christian nation."[4] Even if these statements do not have legal force, the idea of the U.S. as a Christian nation is accepted by very many Americans who justify the presence of religion in their public school system.

Religious Teaching and Practice in Public Schools

Prominent religious educators, such as President Henry P. Van Dusen of the Union Theological Seminary, subscribe to the belief

---

[2] William W. Brickman, "Chronological Outline of Church-State Relations in American Education," in Brickman and Lehrer, *op. cit.*, pp. 254–63.

[3] *Vidal v. Girard's Executors*, 2 Howard 127 (1844).

[4] *Church of the Holy Trinity v. United States*, 143 U.S. 457 (1892).

that it is Constitutional for public schools and colleges to offer "wide variety of religious instruction and religious worship." [5] Another Protestant leader stated that publicly supported institutions may teach nonsectarian religion "in various ways" and "to the full extent" allowable by "state law and public opinion." [6]

So far as practice is concerned, there are numerous studies and reports which offer pertinent information. In 1957, the Michigan State University Commitee on Church Related Programs disclosed that some prayers were recited in half of the public elementary and high schools of the state and that varying percentages of the schools practiced Bible reading and hymn singing—with no law or "legal prejudice" to prohibit "sectarian influences in public schools in Michigan." [7] Several years later, the attorney general of Michigan issued a ruling to ban the long-established religious services carried on in the public schools of the southern part of the state by evangelistic societies.

An examination of the attitude of the Kentucky Court of Appeals revealed that it upheld the Kentucky Constitution of 1792 in prohibiting public school funds for sectarian purposes and sectarian instruction in the public schools. And yet, this court allowed Bible reading, prayers, hymns, and "many Protestant nonsectarian practices" in the public schools. [8] Another research worker recently discovered similar practices in existence in varying degrees in public schools all over the United States. [9]

It will be instructive to review the relevant U.S. Supreme Court decisions of recent years. In 1948, the Court, while insisting that the wall of separation "must be kept high and impregnable," prohibited the teaching of religion during time released from regular classes in public schools. Associate Justice Felix Frankfurter main-

---

[5] Henry P. Van Dusen, *God in Education* (New York: Charles Scribner's Sons, 1951), p. 118.

[6] Merrimon Cuninggim, *The College Seeks Religion* (New Haven, Conn.: Yale University Press, 1947), p. 130.

[7] Robert T. Anderson, "Religion in the Michigan Public Schools," *School and Society*, Vol. 87 (May 9, 1959), p. 228.

[8] Robert L. Collier, *Education, Religion, and the Kentucky Court of Appeals* (Lexington, Ky.: College of Education, University of Kentucky, 1960) pp. 139–40.

[9] Richard B. Dierenfeld, *Religion in American Public Schools* (Washington, D.C.: Public Affairs Press, 1962); and "The Extent of Religious Influence in American Public Schools," *Religious Education*, Vol. LVI (May–June, 1961), p. 167.

tained that "separation means separation, not something less," while the lone dissenter, Associate Justice Stanley Reed insisted coopera- tion between the schools and a lay council of religious education was not forbidden by the First Amendment.[10] Four years later, the Court upheld the reading of Old Testament verses in the public schools in the Doremus Case [11] and, in the Zorach Decision, per- mitted released-time religious instruction on school time, but only outside the public school buildings. Significantly, Associate Justice William O. Douglas remarked that "we are a religious people whose institutions presuppose a Supreme Being," while Associate Justice Hugo L. Black warned that what the majority of the Court approved was "not separation but combination of Church and State." [12] In the most recent decision, the Regents Prayer Case in New York State, decided June 25, 1962, the Court ruled by a six to one vote that the officially written, nonsectarian prayer in the public schools was "an establishment of religion" forbidden under the First Amend- ment. In his concurring opinion, Justice Douglas hinted that other practices, such as free school transportation, school lunches, and textbooks, could also be called into question.[13] In June, 1963, the U.S. Supreme Court declared that the reading of Bible verses and the Lord's Prayer in the public schools was unconstitutional (Schempp and Murray Cases). The public reaction was not one of universal satisfaction.

Public Aid to Parochial Schools:
Pros and Cons

The argumentation over the various phases of church-state school relations has been going on for some time. There are numerous books, pamphlets, and articles. The one aspect of the issue which has probably received the most attention in recent years is the matter of the allotment of public funds for private religious schools. In the following pages, the main contentions which favor and oppose such aid will be presented.[14]

---

[10] *McCollum v. Board of Education,* 333 U.S. 203 (1948).

[11] *Doremus v. Board of Education,* 342 U.S. 429 (1952).

[12] *Zorach v. Clauson,* 343 U.S. 306 (1952).

[13] *Engel v. Vitale,* Supreme Court of the United States, No. 468, October Term, 1961 and June 25, 1962.

[14] For a more detailed analysis, see William W. Brickman, "The Debate over Public Aid to Religious Schools," in Brickman and Lehrer, *op. cit.,* pp. 111–43.

1. The defenders of public aid to parochial education often stress what they call "double taxation"; that is, parents pay their taxes for the public schools and then the expenses for sending their children to a parochial school. They regard this situation as a hardship and as a discriminatory practice, since the parochial school performs the same, if not identical, service as the public school. Moreover, they argue, graduates of parochial schools contribute to the culture, education, welfare, and security of the United States.

Those who oppose public assistance maintain that the law does not compel parents to send their children to religious schools. Should a parent desire to avoid the double taxation, all he has to do is to register them in a public school. Nor are the opponents unduly worried by the possibility that the closing of some parochial schools may throw the public school system in a given community out of balance for some time.

2. Some persons state that public support for religious schools is contrary to the American tradition of taxation for public schools only. The reply is that both the federal and state governments provided funds to sectarian schools for about 150 years after the adoption of the U.S. Constitution. On the other hand, it might be said that the instances of such support were for purposes other than religion. Thus, the federal grants to Negro religious schools intended to aid the education of a people which had been denied schools in a society of slavery. Yet, cannot the same principle be applied, ask those in favor of public funds, to the promotion of education in parochial schools today?

3. The most frequent argument, apparently, is the one that considers public support as violative of the "establishment of religion" clause in the First Amendment. Among those who have argued thus are President Kennedy, laymen of all faiths, and many Protestant and Jewish clergy. The contrary viewpoint says that the Constitution is not specific on the "wall of separation between church and state," and that there have been many violations in American history. If funds have been given in the past and if religion is taught in the public schools, then there has been no complete separation; and, as Justice Frankfurter remarked in the McCollum Case, "Separation means separation, not something less." The opponents claim, however, that breaches in the "wall of separation" have not broken it down and that further breaches should be prevented at all costs.

4. There is fear of public control of religious schools once subsidies are granted. Proponents of public aid reply that there has been no record of federal control of aid to public education and that there already exists supervision and control of all private education by the state authorities.

5. It is also claimed that church and state do not mix in a democracy. This is countered by reference to past and present cooperation between religion and government in many ways, and by the fact that there is public aid to religious schools in such democracies as Great Britain and Holland and none in such nondemocratic countries as the Soviet Union.

6. Many persons feel that the allocation of federal and state money to the parochial schools will weaken and possibly endanger the existence of the public school system. They say that all denominations will want a share of the funds and will expand their religious school programs, thus resulting in the fragmentation of American education. On the other hand, those who favor aid do not fear the demise of the public schools, since some religious groups (the Baptists, for example) oppose parochial schools in any case. Further, some competition might be healthy for the public school, which, according to the Oregon Decision by the U.S. Supreme Court, is not the sole educator of the children and youth of America.

7. Parochial schools should not be publicly financed because they tend to segregate children from the rest of the community. Such divisiveness can be detrimental to a democratic society; yet, the separation of the children is only during school hours. Moreover, some public schools are homogeneous in race, social class, and religion, while many parochial schools are pluralistic in racial, ethnic, and socio-economic respects.

8. Opponents of public aid further assert that the provision of one type of grant will act as an opening wedge for other subsidies. Some might object to free bus transportation, secular textbooks, and lunches, which have been approved by the U.S. Supreme Court and Congress. The contrary argument is that whatever is legal should be made available to parochial schools and that any additional requests will have to be judged on their merits.

9. There is much fear that public support would strengthen the Catholic Church, which would be the major beneficiary because of the extent of its parochial school system. Catholic schools teach

some content which is objectionable to other faiths. Aid, however, will be offered to all religious schools, and the public and the other religious schools also include course material to which other faiths and various nonreligious groups may object.

10. Another argument against public subsidies is that the freedom of religion is thereby placed in jeopardy. Religious freedom, according to this viewpoint, is only safe when church and state are separate. The parochial schools, upon receiving state money, violate the doctrine of separation and endanger the position of their respective faiths in American society. On the other hand, it might be claimed that, because of the breaches in and violations of the wall of separation, there is no freedom of religion in the United States.

11. Fredom of religion, say proponents of federal help, involves a freedom of choice of school, but there is no choice for a parent who cannot afford the fees in many parochial schools. The opponents maintain, however, that the law requires him to send his child to a school, and, if he selects the parochial school, he must provide the necessary funds himself. A person who does not like the public facilities, such as a swimming pool, cannot ask for a subsidy for one of his choosing, in the name of freedom.

12. No citizen, it is argued, should have to be taxed in support of parochial schools which teach doctrines alien to his beliefs. If he is taxed, then he should have a voice in the policies of those schools. Yet, the public pays taxes which, in part, compensate the government for the tax-free churches, but it has no voice in the management of these churches.

13. It will be possible, if funds are given to parochial schools, for sponsors of racial segregation to send their children to private parochial schools closed to Negroes and supported by federal funds. In this way, racially segregated education will be promoted. Public funds, however, have long been allocated to racially segregated public schools in the South, despite the decisions by the U.S. Supreme Court. The extension of segregation to parochial schools can be avoided by the passing of a law denying funds to any parochial school which denies access to qualified Negro pupils.

14. There is fear that new political parties will result from any policy to grant public money to parochial schools. These political groups will use pressure to gain the best advantage for the schools

which they represent. There might even be a conflict among the religious political parties, with a consequent danger to national harmony and unity. On the other hand, no political parties were formed when support in bus transportation, secular textbooks, and school lunches was made available. Nor were new parties organized as a result of the controversies over Bible reading, released time, prayers, and the like.

15. Since the public schools have been publicly supported institutions where Protestant religious doctrines have been taught and religious practices have been in effect, and since the parochial schools have served a public purpose, there has been a dim line of demarcation between both types of schools. If one receives funds from the government, so should the other, since the differences are of degree only. The American people would like to keep religion in the public schools, but they would also like to keep parochial schools from getting tax funds. It is not fair to insist on having the cake and eating it at the same time. In reply, it might be said that the presence of religion in the public schools is a temporary matter. The federal courts have already begun to show their disapproval of some of the practices. In time, the rest would disappear as well. Even with some vestiges of religion, the public school is a vastly different institution from the parochial school.

Over-all View

There does not seem to be any easy solution to this controversial issue. The probability of provision of public funds for parochial schools is remote at present. The proponents of such support will continue to meet heavy opposition in the issue of general federal aid to public education. Perhaps the impasse might be cleared by some sort of compromise.

CHAPTER VIII

The Controversy Over Racially Segregated Education

The issue of the segregation of the races in the public schools of a significant portion of the U.S. is an outstanding one on both the national and the international levels. As a national question, it has had much political and social significance, while internationally it has affected America's reputation and relations abroad. It is not too much to say that the foreign good will toward the U.S. is in direct proportion to the quality of the reforms to assure the Negroes an equal opportunity in education.

Background of the Issue

Immediately after the Civil War, the various states developed differing policies with regard to the education of the Negro in their public schools. Some, like Georgia and Texas, passed laws providing schools for white children only; others, Florida and North Carolina, made legal provision for racially segregated schools; still others, such as Louisiana and South Carolina, ordered integration in education to be incorporated in their constitutions. Outside the South, Nevada authorized separate but equal schools in 1867, as did Indiana in 1869. Michigan (1867) and Connecticut (1868) passed laws which required the policy of racial integration in the public schools. In 1868, the Supreme Court of Iowa prohibited separate schools on state constitutional grounds, while in the following year the Michigan Supreme Court upheld the law of 1867 opening all public schools to Negroes.

During the 1870's, the pattern of segregated public education began to emerge. There seemed, however, to be no clear policy in the nation, except in the South. Thus, in 1874 the Indiana Supreme Court upheld the school segregation law while the Illinois Supreme Court invalidated a similar act. In the 1880's, more Northern states,

New York and Pennsylvania for instance, passed laws against segregated schools. The law (1887) in Ohio was circumvented in some parts of the state by gerrymandering. Interestingly, in the state of California, the Supreme Court in 1885 ordered Mongolian and Chinese children to attend separate schools wherever possible, and the Indian pupils were brought under this law in 1893.[1]

The most important development in the area of racial relations affecting education in the twentieth century was the *Plessy v. Ferguson* decision handed down by the U.S. Supreme Court in 1896. In this case,[2] where railroad transportation facilities were involved, the Court gave official recognition to the doctrine that separate but equal facilities satisfy the requirements of the Fourteenth Amendment's clause on "equal protection of the laws." The minority opinion by Associate Justice John Marshall Harlan is interesting in view of later events: "Our Constitution is color-blind, and neither knows nor tolerates classes among citizens." For close to half a century, this decision was cited as precedent in cases concerned with racial segregation in public education. That the idea of separate but equal facilities might not always be taken literally was evident from a U.S. Supreme Court decision in 1899 which upheld the school-segregation laws of Georgia to the effect that a white high school could be maintained by public funds even if there was no Negro public school in the community.[3]

In the early twentieth century, the Kentucky state law (1904) ordering segregation in education was supported in 1908 by the U.S. Supreme Court in a case affecting a private, church-related college.[4] The result was that the college had to exclude Negro students. Another decision by the highest court of the land upheld the school segregation laws of Mississippi when it held that a Chinese-American child was "colored" and could, consequently, be forced to go to a Negro school.[5]

By 1935, the racial situation in public education appeared to be

---

[1] For an overview of the historical development of the issue, see William W. Brickman, "Chronological Outline of Racial Segregation and Integration in U.S. Schools," in William W. Brickman and Stanley Lehrer, eds. *The Countdown on Segregated Education* (New York: Society for the Advancement of Education, 1960), pp. 152–65.

[2] *Plessy v. Ferguson,* 163 U.S. (1896).

[3] *Cumming v. County Board of Education,* 175 U.S. 528 (1899).

[4] *Berea College v. Commonwealth of Kentucky,* 211 U.S. 45 (1908).

[5] *Gong Lum v. Rice,* 257 U.S. 78 (1927).

hard and fast in the South and in some sections in the North. The education of the Negro pupils was certainly separate from that of the whites, but there was no similar assurance as to equality. Beginning with 1936, a dent began to be made in the solid front of racially segregated schools. A Negro was admitted in 1936 to the University of Maryland Law School after a decision by the Maryland Court of Appeals. In 1938, the U.S. Supreme Court ordered the admission of a Negro student to the University of Missouri Law School in the absence of a separate state law school for Negroes and in view of the fact that an out-of-state scholarship did not constitute an equal opportunity. A Federal Court of Appeals ruled in 1940 that, under the "due process" and the "equal protection" clauses of the Fourteenth Amendment, public school Negro teachers in Norfolk, Virginia, must receive the same salaries as white teachers if their qualifications, experience, and duties are the same. The U.S. Supreme Court denied a writ of *certiorari,* or a review of this decision. Thus, when World War II was imminent, there were two signs on the horizon: the insistence on equality and the beginnings of desegregation.

During World War II, there were instances of racial integration in the armed forces and in defense plants. The North Carolina legislature was the first to pass a law in the South, voluntarily, for the equalization of the salaries of Negro and white teachers. After the War, events began to move with greater speed and frequency on the front of race relations in education. In 1947, Archbishop (now Cardinal) Joseph E. Ritter ordered that the Catholic schools in the archdiocese of St. Louis be integrated, the first such step by any school system in this area. The year 1948 was a very momentous one in the development of the racial issue. The University of Delaware (a border state, but segregated) declared its readiness to enroll Negroes in courses not offered by the Delaware State College for Negroes. One Negro was admitted to the law school and another to the medical school of the University of Arkansas. Moreover, the U.S. Supreme Court ruled that a qualified Negro woman student had to receive a legal education in the state of Oklahoma, and, since there was no separate law school available for Negroes, she was to be admitted to the Law School of the University of Oklahoma. Finally, in 1948 President Harry S. Truman issued an executive order to the effect that "equality of treatment and opportunity" should be granted as soon as possible to all in the armed services "without regard to race, color, religion, or national origin."

Another important year was 1950, when the U.S. Supreme Court ordered Negro students admitted to the University of Texas Law School and the University of Oklahoma Graduate School. It was apparent that the barriers to Negro admission to graduate and professional schools were crumbling in the South. Three years later, Bishop Vincent S. Waters of Raleigh, North Carolina, ordered the desegregation of Catholic schools, churches, and hospitals in his diocese. These events turned out to be barometers of the final breakdown of the legal basis for school segregation. This took place on May 17, 1954, when the U.S. Supreme Court handed down a unanimous decision in several cases striking down the principle of racially segregated public schools, thus overruling the *Plessy v. Ferguson* decision. The conclusion of the Court was that "in the field of public education the doctrine of 'separate by equal' has no place" and that "separate education facilities are inherently unequal." In other words, even if the physical facilities of the Negro and the white school be equal, the very practice of segregation has "a detrimental effect" upon the Negro pupils. "The impact is greater when it has the sanction of the law; for the policy of separating the races is usually interpreted as denoting the inferiority of the Negro group." [6] The outcome of this precedent-shattering decision was the onset of public school desegregation in the fall of 1954 in portions of Missouri, Arkansas, and West Virginia, and in the cities of Washington, Baltimore, and Wilmington. This was done on a voluntary basis, since the Supreme Court did not order the desegregation of any particular public school. Recognizing the "considerable complexity" of the individual cases of segregation brought to its attention, the Court requested further argument by the interested parties in order to help it formulate particular decrees.

On May 31, 1955, after hearing the reargument in the same five cases, the U.S. Supreme Court ordered the federal district courts to require "the defendants to make a prompt and reasonable start toward full compliance with our May 17, 1954 ruling" and undertake the "necessary and proper" measures to make certain that Negro children were admitted to the public schools "on a racial

---

[6] Quoted in *Brown, et al. v. Board of Education of Topeka, Shawnee County, Kansas, et al.,* 347 U.S. 483 (1954).

non-discriminatory basis with all deliberate speed." The federal district courts were charged with the responsibility of determining, in the light of the local situations, whether the plans proposed by the public school systems were adequate "to effectuate a transition to a racially non-discriminatory school system." [7] In brief, the Supreme Court did not order an overnight revolution, but rather a gradual change. According to a legal expert, "The Supreme Court has taken an almost neutral, above-the-battle position, offering approval and gentle encouragement to plans for desegregation without imposing penalties upon those school districts which believe that their time of decision has not yet come." [8]

This gradual approach seemed justified by some in the light of what took place in the following years. In 1956, there were incidents of violence in protest against integration in Mansfield, Texas; Clinton, Tennessee; and Clay and Sturgis, Kentucky. As if these were not enough, during the following year there erupted violence in Little Rock, Arkansas, when local citizens tried to prevent the integration of Central High School. The reverberations of this event were heard all over the U.S. and in every country of the world. In a more peaceful way, some states, like Virginia and Alabama, passed laws in an effort to prevent or limit integration. The struggle for racial equality in the public schools of the South went on in the state and federal courts in the 1950's and the early 1960's. The most dramatic development of this time was the beginning in 1960 of a series of sit-down strikes and other demonstrations of protest by Negro high school students in the South against various forms of segregation. This movement was indicative of the impatience of the Negro at the slow rate of desegregation, which amounted to about one per cent per year in the Southern public schools since 1954.

Current Situation in the South

The Southern Education Reporting Service, a fact-finding group made up of individuals on both sides of the integration issue, announced in December, 1962, that out of a total of 3058 Southern

[7] *Brown, et al. v. Board of Education of Topeka, et al.,* 349 U.S. 294 (1955).

[8] Robert B. McKay, "The Legal Status of School Integration," in Brickman and Lehrer, eds., *The Countdown on Segregated Education* (New York: Society for the Advancement of Education, 1960), p. 85.

districts in which Negro and white pupils attended, 972 public school districts were desegregated. The 255,367 Negro children in the integrated public elementary and high schools constituted 7.8 per cent of the entire Negro pupil population. This figure was an increase of 8379, or two-tenths of one per cent, over that for the spring of 1962. Since 1954, when the first U.S. Supreme Court decision against segregation was handed down, the rate of integration in the seventeen Southern states and the District of Columbia proceeded at the rate of less than one per cent per year. The states with the largest number of desegregated public school districts were Missouri (203), Oklahoma (195), Texas (174), and Kentucky (150). Georgia and Louisiana had one integrated district each, while Alabama, Mississippi, and South Carolina were the only states in which there was no integration at all in the public school system. By way of comparison, 165 out of 292 Southern colleges and universities had admission policies on an integrated basis. The only state which does not admit Negroes to the public colleges and universities is Alabama. Some degree of college faculty integration was prevalent in nine states and the District of Columbia.[9]

It was significant that the scholastic year 1961–62 was the first since 1954 in which there was no violence over the issue of racial integration in public elementary and secondary education. Also of great interest was the inauguration of racially integrated Catholic parochial schools in New Orleans, after an unsuccessful attempt was made by segregationist Catholic laymen to prevent Archbishop Joseph F. Rummel from carrying out his plan.

"De Facto Segregation" in the North

In recent years, a campaign was started by the National Association for the Advancement of Colored People and other groups against the de facto segregation, or separate schools arising out of segregated housing in urban areas, in the North and West. The NAACP resolved in 1961 to oppose Northern school segregation by all available means. During 1961 and 1962, law suits were in-

---

[9] Southern School News, Vol. 9 (December, 1962), pp. 1, 15. See also United States Commission on Civil Rights, Civil Rights U.S.A.: Public Schools, Southern States, 1962 (Washington, D.C.: Government Printing Office, 1962).

stituted in large cities and small communities in New York, Massachusetts, Pennsylvania, Ohio, Illinois, Kansas, California, and other Northern states to bring about a balanced enrollment in the public schools.[10] In December, 1961, the U.S. Supreme Court refused to review a decision by a federal district court ordering the school board of New Rochelle, New York, to end the *de facto* segregation in its public schools. Sit-in demonstrations in a public school in Chicago and in the city hall of Englewood, New Jersey, in 1962 dramatized the growing protest against this form of school organization. The publication of a report *Slums and Suburbs* by Dr. James Bryant Conant, who criticized the new practice of token integration of schools by transporting pupils by bus from one district to another, led to complaints that this educator was trying to retard the process of integration in the public schools of the North. What Dr. Conant urged, instead of *de facto* desegregation, was the immediate improvement of the public schools in the slum areas, which the Negro population usually inhabit.

Private Schools and
the Circumvention of Desegregation

Some of the Southern states, such as Virginia and Louisiana, have undertaken the actual operation, with public subsidies, of segregated private schools in order to circumvent the legal order of integration in public education. Other states—North Carolina, Georgia, and Alabama—also have laws to this effect, but actual tuition payments were made, as of the fall of 1962, only by Georgia. The people of Virginia passed a resolution on January 9, 1956, to amend the state constitution to permit the expenditure of public funds for "nonsectarian private schools." One of the schools which was set up to take advantage of this legal provision, the Tidewater Academy of Norfolk, stated in its objectives that it would "provide

---

[10] Among the charges against public school officials in Northern and Western cities were "gerrymander of school zone lines, transfer policies and practices, discriminatory feeder pattern of elementary to secondary schools, overcrowding of predominantly Negro schools and underutilization of schools attended by whites; site selection to create or perpetuate segregation, discrimination in vocational and distributive education programs in the employment and assignment of Negro teachers." United States Commission on Civil Rights, *Civil Rights U.S.A.: Public Schools, Cities in the North and West, 1962* (Washington, D.C.: Government Printing Office, 1962), pp. 1–2.

Christian education and the observance of prayer and Christian principles as an essential part of its program." [11] It should be noted that here is a case which raises the question of church-state cooperation in education. It is noteworthy that the people of Virginia, especially the sponsors of the Tidewater Academy, are in all probability committed to the principle of separation of church and state, but this does not appear to prevent them from allotting money for what is in effect a parochial school. An estimate by an educator who studied the question of the opening of private schools in the South "for the sole purpose of avoiding desegregation" indicated that, during 1962–63, some 14,000 white pupils in private schools would receive reimbursement from tax funds in the states of Georgia, Louisiana, and Virginia.[12] This specialist, former president of the George Peabody College for Teachers, concludes that if the purpose of the private schools is an emergency measure to avoid the "worse evil" of "mob violence," then the public subsidy of private, segregated education is justifiable; but if "the more than $5,000,000 already expended to support private schools in Virginia is a mere starter in the support of private education, protagonists of public education must oppose such a movement." [13]

Over-all View

The history of racial segregation in American public education is a long one. The trend toward opening the schools of the South to all without regard to race or color has been going on at a rate of about one per cent per annum since the momentous decision of the U.S. Supreme Court in 1954. There has been much resistance and a great deal of token integration. It appears likely, to judge from the events of the early 1960's, that the Negro and other citizens who oppose racial segregation in the public schools will put on increased pressure to force public education in the South to conform to the letter and spirit of the U.S. Constitution as interpreted by the U.S. Supreme Court. Even more, as other actions have recently shown, the campaign to end what is described as *de facto* segregation in the

[11] Preamble of Tidewater Educational Foundation, Inc., By-laws, as quoted in Henry H. Hill, *Public Funds for Private Schools?* (Nashville, Tenn.: George Peabody College for Teachers, 1962), p. 18.

[12] *Ibid.*, pp. 25–26.

[13] *Ibid.*, p. 28.

public schools of the North and West will probably be intensified in years to come. It is hazardous, of course, to venture a prediction, but it is likely that the struggle will continue for some time to come. With increased pressures in Asia and Africa for the rapid equalization of the opportunities of the emerging nations with the older countries in the international scene, it is doubtful if the American Negro and his supporters will remain content with a public school system in any part of the U.S. which does not grant all children an equal chance to develop their potentiality.

CHAPTER IX

The Dual System of American Education

Whenever anyone thinks of the American educational system, it is inevitable for him to consider it as synonymous with the public schools. On the other hand, when higher education is discussed, it is equally inevitable to think of two types, the private and the public. From the standpoint of history, privately supported elementary and secondary schools had their very beginning at the time of the early settlements in the seventeenth century. As time went on, there were two general kinds of education on all levels. Consequently, it is odd that most people, including writers on education, tend to overlook the existence of a system of education which, although reaching relatively small numbers and being financed from non-public sources, has left an imprint on the education, society, and culture of the United States.

The American public schools and the American independent schools have developed together, although at different rates and to vastly differing sizes. The public school has truly endeavored to teach all that could be taught. Even if there have been deviations from the democratic ideal of the establishment of schools for all the children of all the people, the fact remains that the public educational enterprise in America has reached millions who would most probably have not had adequate schooling in other countries. Above all, the American public high school has become an educational institution, the likes of which cannot be found anywhere else in the world. For all its demonstrated faults, the public high school of the United States has turned out to be an educational phenomenon which has been attracting the attention of even the skeptical nations as some sort of a model for the expansion of secondary educational opportunities for young people. Although very little has been said about higher education in this volume, the relatively easy availability of advanced learning to large numbers of the population is another characteristic of the desire by Americans to set up new traditions of flexibility to replace inaccessability or limited access to higher institutions.

It is obvious that the private school system cannot claim the attainments of the public educational enterprise. Independent schools have flourished in Great Britain, on the Continent, and elsewhere in the world. The significance of the English "public" (privately supported) school has perhaps been unparalleled in history, and the American counterparts cannot be said to have exerted a similar influence in the United States. However, the independent schools of various types in America have made a signal contribution to the total educational effort and achievement of the nation. Those who attended the preparatory boarding schools, the military academies, the parochial schools of the various religious groups, the experimental schools, and the various other kinds of independent institutions have not only enriched the country with their particular talents, but they have also added an additional aspect to the pluralism of the American people. When we keep in mind the fact that the independent school has been granted Constitutional status, then it is quite justifiable to speak of another system of schools which is parallel to the public school system. In brief, it is correct to characterize the educational system of America as a dual system.

The peculiar contribution of the religiously oriented private school should be singled out for particular attention. Church-related schools have been able to add an emphasis on moral and spiritual teachings rooted in the Bible and the Western religious traditions identified with Judaism and Christianity. This they have been able to do with freedom in a democratic society which was dedicated to the separation of church and state and did not, therefore, encourage officially such teachings in the public school system. But, as the evidence shows, very many public schools did include religion in some way in their programs, generally under the label of nonsectarianism. Accordingly, the precise identification between the publicly and the privately supported schools tended to become rather hazy. It is, consequently, all the more reasonable to refer to the dual American educational *system*.

As a special form of independent education and as the most widely attended non-public school, the Catholic parochial school has attracted much notice, especially from its critics. Many are very worried over the rise in attendance in recent years. As the

National Catholic Education Association statistics point out, public elementary and secondary school enrollments went up by 42 per cent between 1940 and 1960, whereas the corresponding Catholic school attendance rose by 119 per cent.[1] To large numbers of professional educators and of the citizenry, this trend is alarming, all the more so when they suspect the Catholics of being poised to raid the public treasury to support their schools. It is well to remember, however, that "parochial school Catholics are as involved in community affairs as anyone else of comparable educational position." [2] Catholic schools, like those of the Protestants and the Jews, are not really independent schools; they are quasi-public or semi-public, because they perform a public service by educating young Americans for a useful life in their communities and in the nation at large, and because they are controlled, even if not supported, by the public educational authorities. These considerations should be reviewed when the question of public aid to schools under private auspices comes up again for discussion and debate.

The history of education in the United States is the history of public *and* independent education. Both elements in the dual school system of America have demonstrated their ability to contribute to the national welfare. Both types of education have their proponents and detractors, and there is justification for praise as well as for criticism of their achievements. Both need strengthening, but not at the expense of each other. The profession of education and the public at large should appreciate the uniqueness of the dual system of education in this country and its potentiality for even greater achievement. In a world of turmoil and uncertainty, of competition and conflict, it is fitting for Americans to confront the national and international situations with a dual system of education in which all who teach children and youth cooperate for the advancement of the nation and of mankind.

---

[1] Winifred R. Long, "Enrollment Growth in a Decade—Public and Catholic Schools," *Bulletin*, National Catholic Education Association, Vol. LVIII (May, 1962), pp. 29–31. In 1960, the Catholic elementary schools enrolled 4,373,422 children, while the Catholic secondary schools taught 880,369 students.

[2] Peter H. and Alice S. Rossi, "Some Effects of Parochial School Education in America," *Daedalus* (Spring, 1961), p. 323.

Bibliography

General Historical Works

Brubacher, John S., *A History of the Problems of Education.* New York: McGraw-Hill, Inc., 1947.

Butts, R. Freeman and Lawrence A. Cremin, *A History of Education in American Culture.* New York: Holt, Rinehart & Winston, Inc., 1953.

Cubberley, Ellwood P., *Public Education in the United States,* rev. ed. Boston: Houghton Mifflin Company, 1934.

Curti, Merle, *The Social Ideas of American Educators.* New York: Charles Scribner's Sons, 1935.

Drake, William E., *The American School in Transition.* Englewood Cliffs, N.J.: Prentice-Hall, Inc., 1955.

Edwards, Newton and Herman G. Richey, *The School in the American Social Order,* 2nd ed. Boston: Houghton Mifflin Company, 1963.

Good, H. G., *A History of American Education,* 2nd ed. New York: The Macmillan Company, 1962.

Gross, Richard E., ed., *Heritage of American Education.* Boston: Allyn and Bacon, Inc., 1962.

Kandel, I. L., *American Education in the Twentieth Century.* Cambridge, Mass.: Harvard University Press, 1957.

Knight, Edgar W., *Education in the United States,* 3rd rev. ed. Boston: Ginn & Company, 1951.

———, *Fifty Years of American Education.* New York: The Ronald Press Company, 1952.

Meyer, Adolphe E., *An Educational History of the American People.* New York: McGraw-Hill, Inc., 1957.

Monroe, Paul, *Founding of the American Public School System.* New York: The Macmillan Company, 1940.

Wiggin, Gladys A., *Education and Nationalism: An Historical Interpretation of American Education.* New York: McGraw-Hill, Inc., 1962.

Historical Source Materials

Brubacher, John S., ed., *Henry Barnard on Education.* New York: McGraw-Hill, Inc., 1931.

Cremin, Lawrence A., ed., Classics in Education Series. New York: Bureau of Publications, Teachers College, Columbia University, 1957 to date. Series includes volumes of sources on Horace Mann (Lawrence A.

Cremin), adult education (C. Hartley Grattan), the Supreme Court and education (David Fellman), and Thomas Jefferson (Gordon C. Lee), and others.

Cubberley, Ellwood P., *Readings in Public Education in the United States.* Boston: Houghton Mifflin Company, 1934.

Knight, Edgar W., *A Documentary History of Education in the South Before 1860.* 5 Vols. Chapel Hill: University of North Carolina Press, 1949–53.

Knight, Edgar W. and Clifton L. Hall. *Readings in American Educational History.* New York: Appleton-Century-Crofts, Inc., 1951.

Monroe, Paul, ed., *Readings in the Founding of the American Public School System.* New York: The Macmillan Company, 1940 (microfilm).

Seybolt, Robert F., *Source Studies in American Colonial Education: The Private School.* Urbana, Ill.: University of Illinois Press, 1925.

Spurlock, Clark, *Education and the Supreme Court.* Urbana, Ill.: University of Illinois Press, 1962.

Woody, Thomas, ed., *Educational Views of Benjamin Franklin.* New York: McGraw-Hill, Inc., 1931.

Some Historical Studies

Cremin, Lawrence A., *The Transformation of the School: Progressivism in American Education, 1876–1957.* New York: Alfred A. Knopf, Inc., 1961.

McCluskey, Neil G., S.J., *Public Schools and Moral Education: The Influence of Horace Mann, William Torrey Harris, and John Dewey.* New York: Columbia University Press, 1958.

Nietz, John A., *Old Textbooks.* Pittsburgh, Pa.: University of Pittsburgh Press, 1961.

Welter, Rush, *Popular Education and Democratic Thought in America.* New York: Columbia University Press, 1962.

Wesley, Edgar B., *NEA: The First Hundred Years.* New York: Harper & Row, Publishers, 1957.

Overviews of American Education

Beach, Fred F. and Robert F. Will, *The State and Education,* Misc. No. 23, U.S. Office of Education. Washington, D.C.: Government Printing Office, 1955.

Bereday, George Z. F. and Luigi Volpicelli, eds., *Public Education in America.* New York: Harper & Row, Publishers, 1958.

Callahan, Raymond E., *An Introduction to Education in American Society,* 2nd ed. New York: Alfred A. Knopf, Inc., 1961.

De Young, Chris A. and Richard Wynn, *American Education,* 5th ed. New York: McGraw-Hill, Inc., 1964.

Hughes, James M., *Education in America.* New York: Harper & Row, Publishers, 1960.

Mayer, Martin, *The Schools*. New York: Harper & Row, Publishers, 1961.

Power, Edward J., *Education for American Democracy: An Introduction to American Education*. New York: McGraw-Hill, Inc., 1958.

Thayer, V. T., *The Role of the School in American Society*. New York: Dodd, Mead, & Co., 1960.

Studies of Controversial Issues

Bestor, Arthur E., *The Restoration of Learning: A Program for Redeeming the Unfulfilled Promise of American Education*. New York: Alfred A. Knopf, Inc., 1955.

Brickman, William W. and Stanley Lehrer, eds., *Religion, Government, and Education*. New York: Society for the Advancement of Education, 1961.

————, *The Countdown on Segregated Education*. New York: Society for the Advancement of Education, 1960.

Clift, Virgil A., Archibald W. Anderson, and H. Gordon Hullfish, eds., *Negro Education in America: Its Adequacy, Problems, and Needs*. New York: Harper & Row, Publishers, 1962.

Ehlers, Henry and Gordon C. Lee, eds., *Critical Issues in Education: An Anthology*, rev. ed. New York: Holt, Rinehart & Winston, Inc., 1959.

Harris, Raymond P., *American Education: Facts, Fallacies, and Folklore*. New York: Random House, 1961.

Koerner, James D., ed., *The Case for Basic Education: A Problem of Aims for Public Schools*. Boston: Little, Brown & Co., 1959.

Lieberman, Myron, *The Future of Public Education*. Chicago: University of Chicago Press, 1960.

Rickover, H. G., *Education and Freedom*. New York: E. P. Dutton & Co., Inc., 1959.

Scott, C. Winfield and Clyde M. Hill, eds., *Public Education under Criticism*. Englewood Cliffs, N.J.: Prentice-Hall, Inc., 1954.

Scott, C. Winfield, Clyde M. Hill, and Hobert W. Burns, eds., *The Great Debate: Our Schools in Crisis*. Englewood Cliffs, N.J.: Prentice-Hall, Inc., 1959.

Woodring, Paul, *A Fourth of a Nation*. New York: McGraw-Hill, Inc., 1957.

Private and Parochial Education

Beach, Fred F. and Robert F. Will, *The State and Nonpublic Schools*, Misc. No. 28, U.S. Office of Education. Washington, D.C.: Government Printing Office, 1958.

Beck, Walter H., *Lutheran Elementary Schools in the United States*. St. Louis, Mo.: Concordia Publishing House, 1939.

Burns, J. A., *The Catholic School System in the United States*. New York: Benziger Bros., Inc., 1908.

Burns, J. A. and Bernard J. Kohlbrenner, *A History of Catholic Education in the United States*. New York: Benziger Bros., Inc., 1937.

Curran, Francis X., *The Churches and the Schools: American Protestantism and Popular Elementary Education.* Chicago: Loyola University Press, 1954.

Dushkin, Alexander M., *Jewish Education in New York City.* New York: Bureau of Jewish Education, 1918.

Dushkin, Alexander M. and Uriah Z. Engelman, *Jewish Education in the United States.* New York: American Association for Jewish Education, 1959.

Grinstein, Hyman B., *The Rise of the Jewish Community of New York, 1654–1860.* Philadelphia: Jewish Publication Society of America, 1947.

Heely, Allan V., *Why the Private School.* New York: Harper & Row, Publishers, 1951.

Private Independent Schools, 15th ed. Wallingford, Conn.: Bunting and Lyon, 1962.

Seybolt, Robert F., *The Private Schools of Colonial Boston.* Cambridge, Mass.: Harvard University Press, 1935.

Sherrill, Lewis J., *Presbyterian Parochial Schools, 1846–1870.* New Haven, Conn.: Yale University Press, 1932.

The Handbook of Private Schools, 43rd ed. Boston: Porter Sargent, 1963.

Index

115